Charity

Fundraising is more than wishing!

To Jody,
You are a jewel!
3-10-10

Best wishes,
Jeanette North

15 Wishes for your success!

Jeanette North

© 2009 by Jeanette North

All rights reserved. No portion of this book may be reproduced, stored in a retrieval system, or transmitted in any form or by any means, electronic, mechanical, photocopy, recording, scanning, or other-except for brief quotations in critical reviews or articles, without the prior written permission of the publisher.

Library of Congress Cataloging –in-Publication Data

North, Jeanette

  Charity genie: fundraising is more than wishing / by Jeanette North

ISBN   978-1-60458-586-5

Book cover by Marce Lewallen of ML Graphics

The sponsoring editor for this book was Norma Walters.

Content of Wishes

Page

Wish One:	*Wishing for Your Success!*	*1*
Wish Two:	*Wishing for MORE Money!*	*9*
Wish Three:	*Wishing for Passion!*	*24*
Wish Four:	*Wishing for the Perfect Package!*	*34*
Wish Five:	*Wishing for Vivacious Volunteers!*	*48*
Wish Six:	*Wishing for Powerful Presentations!*	*70*
Wish Seven:	*Wishing for a Political Pelican!*	*90*
Wish Eight:	*Wishing for a Queen Bee to Network!*	*110*
Wish Nine:	*Wishing for a Marketing Guru!*	*126*
Wish Ten:	*Wishing for More Fun in Fundraising!*	*148*
Wish Eleven:	*Wishing for the Free!*	*158*
Wish Twelve:	*Wishing for Spectacular Events!*	*172*
Wish Thirteen:	*Wishing for a Better Board!*	*194*
Wish Fourteen:	*Wishing for a Miracle!*	*204*
Wish Fifteen:	*Fundraising is More Than Wishing!*	*212*
About the Author		*216*

All events are based on true stories. Some of the names, locations, and other details have been changed to protect the identity of the humble, innocent, and a few guilty parties.

Fundraising is more than wishing!

Jeanette North jnorthstar@msn.com
P. O. Box 674 Cell (918) 902-1154
Owasso, OK 74055 * www.charitygenie.com

A **$5 donation or 10%* from the purchase price** of this book will be made **to the 501c3 charity of your choice**. If no request is made, the author will choose a charitable beneficiary. *Some restrictions do apply.

Disclaimer: Please note that although these are proven techniques and results received by the author, they are not guaranteed due to variations of application.

DEDICATION

This book is dedicated to my father,

Marvin M. Hendrix

July 28, 1931-September 13, 2008

"Gone fishing"

ACKNOWLEDGMENT

Special acknowledgement goes to all the charity workers and volunteers that struggle daily to make a difference in the lives of others and our society. You are the true heroes!

I would like to acknowledge Ron, my husband, for his love and willingness to support the writing of this book. My friend, Norma Walters, was so very kind to edit and improve my work. My dear sweet friends, Brenda, Donna Ann, GiGi, Margaret, Melanie, Monica, and others encouraged me along the way. I would like to acknowledge Kayla, Vickie, and all the people who have touched my life and whose stories are woven on the pages.

Mentors are vital to the growth of each individual and they are not always who you would expect. They come in all shapes-and-sizes, such as, the homeless woman, high-society redhead, well-dressed prisoner, single mom with teen girls, and many others. Konnie Boulter, Diana D., Jim Stovall, and others took me under their wings to nurture and guide me.

Our two grown sons, Ryan and Kyle, and their families including our grandchildren, Rhett, Rylie, and Caitlyn are the joys of my life. Our pugs, Baxter, Gracie, and Taz-Bo keep us laughing with their cute little faces and remind me to play.

"Thank you" one and all for your love and support. I truly am a blessed woman, whose biggest task in life is simply to help others!

Love and Best Wishes,

Wish One

Wishing for your Success!

If wishes for your success were all that it took, I would send you the biggest wish of all for your charity's success. If I could just blink my eyes and nod my head and all financial dreams for your charity would come true, I would! Don't get me wrong, you can succeed, but it will take more than wishing. The hope of a huge foundation giving you that 1.2 million dollar annual gift-could happen. Your dreams of a big name donor presenting you with a big check on the front page of the newspaper-could happen. Maybe an order of nuns in Texas will send you a substantial five figure donation in the mail. Oh! Wait! That did happen. My true wish for you is that some of my personal experiences will parlay into additional funds in your bank account for achievement of total potential fulfillment of your mission.

Wouldn't it be nice, if a genie could grant you a new pair of designer sunglasses and you would really be able to take a fresh look at your charity! These glasses would reveal what others really see from their perspective. Remember, "I can't think like you do, and you can't think like I do." It sounds like such an easy concept, but communication is the major cause of most misconceptions of everything from vision to end services. Before you are ready to ask for money, you will need 1) a good product and 2) to know how to ask for a commitment. Is your product (charity) structured and professional? Do you have a Marketing and Organizational Plan in place? You may say that you are small and it doesn't matter, but it does. Do you know how to barter for what you need, that cost money you don't have? How do you treat your volunteers, or do you even have trusted and loyal volunteers? How is your networking in the community with foundations, corporations, civic, churches, potential donors, media, politicians and other social organizations? Are you still trying to raise serious money with a lot of bake sales, car washes, or garage sales, instead of high-profile annual events? These not only serve as fundraisers, but friend raisers and reasons for the media to promote your charity. The "Fun Factor" is so vital that it is the first three letters in *fun*draising. You need to contemplate and answer these questions, and you may just discover how to create an ample supply of money for your most important mission of caring for others!

Complete chapters are devoted to each of these questions and concerns. "Jeanette, wait just a minute, we have all purchased this book to learn more about fundraising!" Yes, but are you ready to fundraise? As I have volunteered and worked for many charities, most are NOT ready! Answer this question? If you went into a grocery store and there was a row of products on display that were exactly the same or very similar, which one would you buy? Would you buy the one with the wrapper bunched up in production or outdated? Would you buy the one without a logo or a list of its contents? No, you probably would pick one in a nice package, with a quality name or a brand that you believed in, or one that your friends said was superior. You would pick a good value at a good price. Charities are like products in the stores. There are so many, many great causes to whom donors can give. Professional charities are giving great value and providing great results for foundations' and donors' valuable investment dollars, so why would they give money to an inferior one?

Let's talk about the word value. The partial mission of a charity that I worked for was to provide counseling services to our community. These services would be made available on a sliding scale payment, to clients who could not afford them. The police station, located across the street, had seen an increasing need for a domestic violence counselor. How could I address this part of our mission? I knew for a fact that one of the major foundations in the nearest metropolitan area had a real heart for this cause and the money to back it up. While reading the newspaper one day, I tore out a prominent article detailing a gift from this foundation. Ironically, later I showed this foundation executive the article, and told her that it was responsible for planting the seed for my venture. A casual conversation with a friend of this founder revealed to me that he was often referred to as "Mr. H" by many homeless clients of a charity that bore his name. This pseudonym obscured the identity of this benefactor of a marvelous daytime shelter. I penned a letter to this man by his endearing nickname and told him of the need for a domestic violence counselor and an additional need for a children's counselor for these families. I explained the basic statistics and the two existing charities that already provided these services. This funding could send counselors to our city as needed beginning with one to two days a week. The current back log for victims was about a one month wait and transportation was an issue, but with this funding, counseling could be provided within a week. This would provide one year of services in our city and three smaller towns in the vicinity, for mostly women of abuse and their children all for $50,000. This number was the amount on the budgets provided by these charities with a small coordination percentage for us. Collaboration with the appropriate proven charities increases your odds of receiving funds and is looked on very favorably. The foundation granted the money.

I recently read in the local newspaper that this money provided 500 domestic violence counseling visits in this first year. The value is showing that citizens in four cities received needed counseling services quickly. Additional services for the children's counseling were not documented in this article. Why would a foundation give this same $50,000 to an organization that could not provide documented statistics and help less than 20 people per year? What could you do with a $50,000 grant? How many people could you help in one year? Could you measure the results and if so, do you currently? At the bottom line, is your charity worthy of this donation, if you were competing for it?

What is the value of your organization through the eyes of your community, potential donors and foundations? In business, two simple rules of thumb are to ask better questions and spend 80% of your time and brain power on the solution and 20% on identifying the problem. Changing a few of your techniques and focusing on solutions can reap big financial benefits for major impact. An old real estate boss and mentor used to tell me daily, "If you always do what you've always done, you'll always get what you always got!" This reached to the point of being a regular annoyance, but I never forgot his lesson, although I'm pretty sure he borrowed the concept from Einstein. What are you willing to change and improve to accelerate your fundraising efforts? If you are experiencing a valley, concentrate on the mountain top just ahead. This will be a fun and exciting journey so jump on the magic carpet, and let's go out there and answer some of these questions and find some gold for your mission! Best wishes for your success!

<u>Wish Two</u>

Wishing for MORE Money!

Please note that nonprofit does not have to mean no money in the bank. Let me sit with you for a moment and hold your hand-metaphorically speaking. You are trying to do the work of three or four people for a mission that you truly believe in. You may even be the founder, but money is a real issue! You definitely have the bank account blues. When needs arrive and bills come due, do you have to think about how those bills will get paid? I ran a charity with money and without money and it was a lot easier with money. You have to look at the reasons why your charity is not prospering. You need to get a few outside opinions or maybe read this book. The problem is you can't always see the problem, but someone else, who has walked in your shoes, may be able too.

After doing some consulting, I see a pattern for why charities and business in general do not succeed. It usually is not just one issue, but a combination of improvements that are necessary. Most people want to get right to the "ask!" They have put off fundraising until their bank account is in the red or at least heading that direction. They expect to hire a consultant and offer them money that they don't have. It is their hopes that this *overpaid* professional will be able to pick up the phone and call their contacts to "save the day!" The consultants did not make the mess, and it is their purpose to help you clean up your own mess. "Ouch! Jeanette, we are just getting to know each other and you're already hitting a sensitive nerve!" Is your mission worth saving? Well then let's put down our egos (no one is looking) and get our eyes and energy on saving this charity!!! I'm still holding your hand and I recognize this ego thing from my own experience. Let's explore what you need to do to get ready for the "ask."

I became familiar with the power of the "ask" at a very young age. One day I went to my grandfather and told him that I wanted to make some money. He was a very wise man although he only had an 8th grade education. He had to quit school to support his mother and four sisters after his father's death. This was a man who went to California during the Oklahoma Dust Bowl. I remember the story of him picking up odd jobs on his way across country because of the hard times. He worked all day putting up a circus tent on a promise that the man would pay him a small amount of money. I believe it was a quarter. At the end of a very hard day of dragging out canvas, hoisting up huge poles and staking down the sides, the man did not pay him a dime. This was the only time my grandmother said that he cried over money. He planned to eat on that money. My grandfather taught me a very important lesson about the value of money and earning it.

Instead of reaching into his pocket, he took me to the co-op and purchased a packet of radish seeds. We worked the soil in a small plot of a vegetable garden on the side of his front yard. He had been a wheat farmer most all of his life after his return to Oklahoma and knew how to grow just about anything. We called his tomatoes "steaks" because they were so big that you only needed one big slice to cover a whole piece of bread for a BLT. We planted the seeds and every day we would tend and water the small plants. The day finally came to harvest our large radishes. He showed me how to clean them and put them in baggies. This was before the invention of zip top sandwich bags. We decided to sell them for a "dime bag" and that was before the current meaning of a "dime bag." I went and got my red wagon and loaded the bottom full of the freshly grown and prepared produce and took off down the street. I went up to my very first door and knocked on it. A man appeared. I said "Would you like to buy some radishes for a dime?" He not only bought one, but bought three. I was HOOKED! You mean that I can walk up to a door and knock on it and people will give me money?

Many charities think, yes this is how it works, but did you notice that I found a mentor, my grandfather. We purchased the seeds for radishes, worked the soil, planted the seeds, monitor our daily progress. We cleaned the radishes and cut off all the unnecessary leaves, roots, and bad spots. Mother donated new baggies and my little red wagon was a mode of transportation to get the finished product to the potential customers. I sold every one of those bags of radishes that day. I don't remember ever growing radishes again, but I have repeated this process many, many times. This lesson has served me well to this day!

One little footnote to this story is my friend and I wanted to earn some money some years later. We lived on a non-working dairy. My dad purchased it just as an investment and place to call home. I took my friend out to our pasture, and we spent all Sunday afternoon picking wild blackberries. We filled up a one gallon milk carton, because these berries were so small with many stickers on the bushes. We decided to sell this carton for $2.00, which meant one dollar for her and one dollar for me for our afternoon of work and splinters. We loaded up the same little red wagon and off we went to visit the banker's wife. Past experiences made me sure that she would purchase our "expensive" berries. I knocked on her door, showed her the wonderful produce and told her they were $2.00. She said that was too much and she would only pay $1.50. This meant that Vickie and I would not get the dollar each that we had planned on. I stayed firm to my price, and the banker's wife stayed firm to her counter offer. I went back and conferred with my business partner. We decided that we would split the blackberries and take them home to our mothers to bake a cobbler for each of our families. I remember it was most delicious blackberry cobbler ever!

"Jeanette, why did you tell us this story?" you may be asking. Well, I took what my grandfather taught me and passed it on to my friend. We worked together and had fun. We tried and "failed", but we took all the right steps and decided the value of our time and efforts. We did not sell ourselves short. Our families enjoyed the fruits of labor and what looked like a "failure" was really a true success. The process was the same.

1. Desire to make some money
2. Find a product (Mission)
3. Work to make it happen

4. Know how much you want to make
5. Find the people that want to buy
6. Knock on the door (make the phone call)
7. Ask for the money
8. Don't sell yourself short

After twenty years in the field of sales and marketing, I have sold everything from modeling courses to water heaters. I have read almost every book about this subject that I could get my hands on, and the "Golden Rule" was the most common thread.

Treat other people how you want to be treated.
Sell a product that you believe in.
Find a need and fill it.
How can I help?

This is gold. These are not only good solid rules for sales and marketing. I found they work really well for life! I know they work and will help your charity raise money!

The genie from an old television show was always granting wishes for her astronaut master. Is your charity skyrocketing? Accelerating to the stratosphere without a genie? Oh! You forgot to take care of your fundraising and now your mission is in serious condition! It may not only stall, but there is a chance that it may fall (go bankrupt)! "This is not only a good mission, it is a **great** mission and I have worked so very hard" you say. Well get ready to stop reading after this next sentence. If you are so very sure that you are right when it comes to fundraising, because you have been so very successful in the mission, please answer this question. What does your bank account say? If the bills are stacking up, you might want to reconsider how you are going to pay for the fuel to operate your skyrocketing charity.

Good charities go out of business everyday due to lack of funding for fuel.

The best advice that I ever discovered is: Never tell a professional how to do his job. I learned this lesson when a professional painter insisted that I meet him at 7 am to discuss the color of paint for our new house. "You said you wanted a beach feel, but if I paint your interior this mother-of-pearl color, it will be pink and you will hate it." I said, "You're the professional!" I knew he was very experienced and knowledgeable. My house was probably on the low-end of homes he had painted. I loved the color and loved the fact that he took the time and his expertise to make sure I was happy. I was thankful that I listened and have never forgotten this lesson. If you do decide to hire a fundraising professional don't tell him how to do his job. Give them the freedom to surprise you with their best work! This is repetitive, but it is worth repeating.

You may be new to fundraising, a seasoned veteran, or just another hat for the Executive Director or Board Member. Fundraising is the sales and marketing division of a charity and the charity is the business. This was the approach that I took as the new ED of a charity that was $10,000 in debt. I volunteered the first month due to the lack of funds and to determine if this was a path that I wanted to take.

I co-own of a small plumbing business with my husband, who has been in business for over 25 years. I have taken leave from the company three times, but we have been married for over 34 years. As I always say, "He deserves a Purple Heart for living with me!" I'm so very thankful that he understands my desire to try new career adventures. I pulled on my knowledge of a time we had to rejuvenate our own company. We were able to triple our profits in one year and achieved 16-19% profit margins in an industry where the average profit margin was 2-3% at the time. We determined the most profitable area for us was in remodel and repair and left the new construction headaches to the larger companies. We streamlined, organized, categorized and focused only on our profit center and, vitally important, we executed a progressive marketing plan. This was not a complex or costly plan, but simply included networking with local businesses and organizations. One of our biggest successes was affiliating with a local utility company. We received co-op advertising dollars and name association with a solid and well recognized corporation. We soon were ranked as the #1 Plumbing Contractor by Public Service Company for their Electric Water Heater Program.

I started thinking what I did before to triple our profits. The first thing to do is take stock of:

- Where is your business now?
- Where has your business been?

What is working?

What or who is dragging your business down? This may be someone you believe to be your friend, but they are sabotaging all your efforts.

- Most of all, where is your business going? What are your goals? How are you going to meet these goals?

Another key to our success was bundling services by coordinating the electrician, plumber, supply house delivery, city inspector and utility company with the homeowner. With one call the homeowner could accept this offer and have concept-to-completion installation within 24 to 48 hours. The paperwork was delivered to the customer's door or workplace for their signature and returned for expedient payment. This resulted in 22 promotions for our company in the short month of February, whereas most of the other companies were promoting 3 to 4 a month. The ability to take a program and simplify it with ease of execution is the key to a successful program, whether it is with a plumbing company or a charity. This is the same process that our charity took for various programs and even dealing with media. Get an easy, workable system by organizing all the participants and paperwork. One phone call can trigger concept-to-completion results, if all the elements, individuals, companies, and paperwork have been set up into a workable system. Media loved that I would totally coordinate a story within an hour or two therefore they would call me often, because it was so easy for them. We received fantastic television and news coverage, often for streamlining their stories.

Preparation is vital to your ability to raise more money. It is very common for me to spend at least a month totally revamping a product or charity, before it is ready for marketing. First of all you need to understand every aspect of your organization or product before you can sell it. It needs to be a product that you believe in and are proud to attach your name. It needs to be organized and updated. Outdated material and programs need to be eliminated. If you and your friends would buy it or donate to it, then it is probably ready to be rolled out to the public. Analyze where you are and where you want to be and then be prepared to roll up your sleeves and work to make this happen! I don't know who said, "Luck is where preparation and opportunity meet!" If you are willing to go that extra mile to prepare your charity for market, money will come. Best wishes for more money!

Notes:_____

_____

_____

_____

_____

Wish Three

Wishing for Passion!

A woman came walking into our reception with two young teenage daughters by her side. This was a rather unusual site. Teens usually don't come with their parents to ask for food. She worked at a local retail store and explained that she was getting paid tomorrow. She said, "I just need food for today!" This is a single mom and a classic example of the working poor. I quickly thought of the gift cards that a local Mexican restaurant had donated for our clients. The girls' eyes lit up and the mom was so very appreciative. We loaded them down with food for about two weeks from the pantry. Her birthday was the next day and they would be able to go out and eat to celebrate. Friends would ask me, "Jeanette, isn't it depressing to work with people with problems all the time?" My response is, "If I could do handsprings to my car every day, I would. It reminds me of how very blessed that I am. I have the opportunity to help them. I was chosen for this job!" This story resonates with passion, and how can a donor resist donating to help this woman, her teen girls, and others like them?

Recently, I read in the obituary that one of my client friends, Phyllis had died. She was such a lovely woman, but in poor health. Every Christmas, I would think, she probably won't be here next year. She told me how her two children had died in their late teens and early twenties due to health issues. She told about the abusive childhood of her husband. She loved life and loved the people around her. One Christmas, her "gifts" of toilet paper, medicated power, soap, dishwashing detergent, gauze, ointment, etc. were lost. Her list was filled with daily essentials. We purchased a second set then her gifts were found. She received a double supply. This was a godsend for all the ways she helped others. She would always say if you need me to do something, let me know. Since she worked at a major discount store, she personally handled and secured the items we needed for various projects.

The floor of her trailer was rotten, and there was a church that wanted a project. We facilitated this match and they rebuilt her floor and replaced her stool. Everything was donated, a real community project. We were even able to give dog food to her poodle, Sadie, and one of the loves of her life. She beamed and lit up the room with her spirit every time she came in, although you could see the pain and suffering of her health in her face and eyes. She inspired me to make sure that we had plenty of food and extras in our pantry for the next time she and all of our clients came in. She sparked my personal passion to make a difference in her life and others. I did that! Yea! A mental handspring just flashed through my mind and a few tears in my eyes. This is passion!

Sidebar: "You can never want more for someone than they want for themselves!" I still have a mental video image of an old realtor that stood up in a meeting and said those very wise words. They have served me well, working with people in need. You can want a better life for others, but they have to want it for themselves. If you think you can make them want it, you are just pig wrestling. As the tale goes, "You will just make them mad and get yourself dirty!"

It is 3 o'clock in the morning and I am sitting up in bed no longer able to delay the withholding of this most vital information of ample supply of money for your mission. There is an organization in Colorado that has a national convention each year in July and this is my first year to attend. I was working with a charity and had the good fortune to discover this most wonderful group of "do gooders!" (Yes, I am aware spell check just redlined me, but it is NOT from Oklahoma.)

The mission of this precious group of people is to care for mostly teenagers that have dropped out of school and have no purpose for their lives. These are not the average public alternative school teens, but the hardcore ones that have fallen through the cracks of society more than once in traditional schools. This group consists of founders, administrators and teachers. Two women have felt this "calling" to open a school within the next two years. One is a kindergarten teacher from Virginia and the other is a fundraiser for a charity serving unwed mothers in Pennsylvania. The majority of these schools are small and their budgets are even smaller!

One woman had worked for four years without a paycheck. She quit an $80K a year job as a Tech

Support for a major corporation, moved out of her five bedroom home to a small two bedroom rental, in order to fulfill her purpose of working with high-risk, underserved, non-traditional teens. She told the story of two young teen boys that had been initiated into different gangs and did not want to be members, so they would sneak off from their gangs and go TO her school. They realized the need for their education. One student was a homeless teen girl. One was a boy that called every high school and no one would take him because of his past, but this one. One boy took a gun to school. One teen's next-of-kin were all in jail. You get the idea. Her own troubled son and his friends were the drivers for her passion.

Most of us are not "called" to be teachers much less teachers of high school age teens with such dramatic problems and histories. It is the love for these children that makes these teachers risk "life and limb" to help. The teachers have heard the stories of neglect and abuse and realize most all of these teens are just a product of their environment. They are on the cycle of poverty circulating just like the hamster on the wheel with no way to get off. Many people say, straighten up, get a job, be responsible. What does that look like? These poor children don't even know! Children only learn what they see and most of these have seen more than "middle" America ever will.

As an Executive Director of a "needs" charity for two small cities, our organization gave people in need food, utility assistance, school supplies, Thanksgiving baskets, Christmas gifts, etc. I called it a "needs" charity, because if anyone needed anything, they would call us. As I would visit with these (mostly) women about what they needed, I would observe the "babies" behind their skirt tails and knew many of them did not have a prayer's chance to break this cycle. In twenty years, I imagined the workers and volunteers' children would be helping the next generation of children of the mostly working poor with food, utility assistance, etc. You get the picture. I got so tired of "putting on Band-aids!" We were happy to be able to meet their need for the day, but knew we had not made an impact on their future past the current month.

The reason that I bring this up is: the people at this organization and the schools that they represent, are helping break this cycle of poverty. For every teenage dropout that they recover from the streets and send on to technology training or college will save our society over a half million dollars over this student's lifetime. WOW! This dollar amount is just a bonus to us, but their bonus is the possibility of a "normal" life. Their possibilities are for a family and a future full of hope that their children someday will be able to complete high school and maybe even graduate from college. Now! This is a positive action that can reduce poverty! Get out your checkbooks!

"Jeanette, I thought this book was about fundraising." Yes, but you have to understand and really feel the passion for the purpose of your mission! If raising money for you is just a job, then this book is probably NOT for you, or you may need to change jobs! Either get out of fundraising or find a mission that gets into your blood! There are a few extra exclamation marks in this paragraph, but I feel very, very strongly about this fact! **Your passion** is one of the major key elements to raising money. This is a very, very important part of finding money for YOUR purpose! Passion sparks action and motivates people to help and give. Feel the love, feel the passion. Write books at 3am! Best wishes for embracing your passion to help others and passing it along to people that can fund your mission!

<u>Wish Four</u>

Wishing for the Perfect Package!

In my twenties, I worked for a very wealthy woman, who taught me much about social etiquette and the power of presentation. She loved to give gifts and shopped only in the most exclusive stores in a very prestigious area. I soon noticed that she might purchase brass candlesticks on sale and spend as much on the gifts bags and tissue. When tactfully questioning her gifting habits, she explained "Oh people love to receive gifts, but it is the thoughtful presentation of the gift and the exquisite wrapping that they enjoy!" "Oh!" I said. She taught me a very important lesson that day. Presentation is everything and with sincerity and attention to detail, presentation is really perception of the total giving experience. This is very critical in the sales and marketing of a product and very critical to your product aka charity. What does your charity look like? What is your image to your donors, community at large, and yes, even your clients?

Quick sidebar, when you are giving to people in need, your clients should feel as if they are receiving a gift and not a handout. I made sure that backpacks were provided for our school supplies and 3 foot felt stocking for the Christmas gifts. The children were thrilled. The following year, it was decided that most were returning clients and backpacks were not necessary for everyone, except upon special request. We received a wonderful donation of large paper grocery sacks decorated with a back-to-school design. I reluctantly agreed to this less than spectacular packaging. They were nice, and I showed them exactly how I wanted them closed for the effect of a gift. Some of the bags looked awful. A portion of volunteers believe that it doesn't matter the quality of their work, since they are not getting paid. Impress upon them nicely that they should put forth their best efforts for others who are experiencing hard times.

How dare you call my passion a product! It is marvelous the plethora of society's problems that charities are addressing. There are many strong visionaries with many good intentions, but they forget due diligence when structuring their organizations. The following is a suggested basic checklist for charities.

- The 501c 3 charitable status
- The proper accreditations and certifications required by their field of service
- Financial recordkeeping can be done with a simple software program and overseen by a CPA. I would recommend a good treasurer on your board for all math challenged EDs' out there!
- A proper business and marketing plan for the next five years.

"Jeanette, what does this have to do with fundraising?" This is foundation building.

The goal is to dissect your charity in every area that relates to organizational structure and marketing efforts and construct a long-term Organizational and Marketing Plan for your future. It should be designed to be easily understood and workable for your organization over the next five years. How does your overall program look? Do you have all of your "ducks in a row?"

What does your organization look like physically? Is it messy and unorganized? Do you collect every old couch given to you and place them all over? Is the paint peeling? Does your building have dirty bathrooms with dead bugs on the floor? This is so common in some of the small charities that I have visited. After all they can't afford a cleaning service and the staff is overloaded. There are very few volunteers that will offer to provide this service on a regular basis.

Image is everything in reference to branding. These are the concerns that need to be addressed and solved before an organization is ready to implement a Strategic Marketing Plan. The facility needs to be de-cluttered, minimized, and organized. Volunteers need to be contacted for a new paint job maybe in a soft, creamy, off-white colored applied to the total interior and renew exterior color. There are professional interior designers who will volunteer a small portion of their time to give you a site review and provide low-cost recommendations for a more professional look. The exterior entry may need a new permanent sign. For example, the interior entry needs to be structured like a reception area with quality furniture and a few pictures. The receptionist, office and records area may need to be cleaned, minimized, organized, and functional. Remove all debris including old couches. Keep all areas cleaned, organized and very professional, so as to project a business atmosphere, but remain relaxed, friendly, and comfortable. A small area can serve as a lounge. The total facility should follow suit to offer a structured and consistent environment.

The atmosphere represents the charity's pride and professionalism. Professionals including painters, remodelers, plumbers, etc. can volunteer their time for this makeover. Please remember to sing their praises to television and newspaper media for their contributions. This provides a form of "payment" and a real willingness to return to future projects and the possibility of becoming on-going monetary donors.

Is your charity professional?

Basic checklist:
- Clean and organize your office and operating space. If you do not have a designated work area, create one.

- Organize your schedule whether it is online or monthly calendar. (Is your schedule booked full of things you enjoy? Ask yourself, does this appointment help achieve my long-term fundraising goals?)
- Do you have a vision, mission, and goals statement?
- Is your website updated? Can donors contribute easily, including a secured online process?
- Are your business cards, brochures, letterhead, envelopes updated and professional?
- Do you have an updated business plan that is workable?
- Do you have an updated marketing and organizational plan that is workable? Do you look at it weekly?

Is your mission (product) sellable?
- Are you trying to do everything? Don't duplicate other services and just try to do a few things well!
- Are you holding onto out dated programs or creating news just for funding?
- Do you know what you need and how much it cost?
- Do you have a budget?
- What is the "Structure of your Ask?" It is clear, concise, and written down including the cost of each item need? ("Ask" is the official request for monetary support.)
- Would you donate to your mission?
- Does everyone on your Board of Directors donate to your mission? Do they even know your mission and contribute their influence and networking strength?
- Are you able to provide the number of clients served, volunteer hours, items

donated and distributed? Start this today, even if it is a log in or sign-up sheet on a clip board with a receipt book in duplicate. Clarity is what your "big picture" looks like. What does your community think about your charity? You must start with this overview and piece it down to size. If all the bridges have been burned by previous Directors, then fundraising will be impossible until these bridges have been rebuilt and all the fences have been mended with your volunteers, foundations, corporations, civic and other groups and offended donors. In sales, this is referred to as a golden opportunity to repair the damage and build even stronger relationships, which can evolve to future funding. Look around; ask questions, and take surveys, but the number one person to sell your charity to….is you. Over twenty years in the field of sales and marketing, I would never sell a product that I would not buy or believe in. Do you believe in your charity?

During my many lives, I was a marketing rep for a large electric utility company. I remember sitting in at a round table meeting and they (mostly men) were discussing the sale of a particular product. I knew for a fact that this product had faulty materials and there was a nationwide lawsuit in the beginning stages. I let this be known to the group and one of the men said, "…but they don't know that!" I said, "Well, I do and we as a company are putting ourselves and others at risk and it will be costly in the long run." This product was withdrawn by the group. I was the rep on this particular product and I would NOT have promoted it, even if it cost me my job.

You will need to evaluate your charity's culture. The culture for this corporation was very foreign to me. I came from small business environments, and this was the first time that I had worked for a large corporation. Our small company had promoted 50% of all this large corporations' electric water heaters, and they had invited me to become one of their marketing reps. As I "swam" through these unfamiliar waters, I noticed that in many roundtable meetings (higher level executives meetings) that it was very common for these executives to determine a particular point-of-view, and that this point-of-view would be released for the company employees to buy into. I remember thinking, if you put a squeeze bottle of mustard and a bottle of ketchup in the middle of that table, and it was so determined that mustard was NOW ketchup and ketchup was NOW mustard. Then this philosophy would be the cultural standard for the employees to "buy into." I determined that I must BELIEVE in a product, not buy into it. Believing in your product aka charity makes your passion sellable!

This is what I would like to ask for you to do. Believe in your charity; don't just "buy into it." If there are areas of your organization that you do not believe in, can they be "fixed" or changed? Boards remind me of these roundtable meetings. Many do not even believe in their own charity. They cannot "sell" them or promote them, because many don't even darken their doors. If you believe and love your charity, your passion will shine through, and others will believe in it too. They will want to donate their time and energy and what we need the most-their money!

The bottom line is to think of your charity in the terms of a complete package in a spectacular wrapping (pink would be my preference with a big gold bow). Use everything from binoculars to the microscope to access the total perception of your charity. You may say that you don't have much money (yet), but you can clean up your facility and clean up your image! I'm not saying to play house, meaning have no substance. I'm saying downsize, categorize, and organize all your programs and facility. Look and act professional and encourage your staff to do the same. Make sure your business cards, website, brochures and forms look professional. Cheaper is not always better. I'm so sick of hearing about amateur web designers that are unskilled and never complete the job, but they're free. No my dear, they are costing you big money, because you are losing out on big sales aka donations.

Beautiful gifts are easily purchased and easily given. Your donors, community, media, corporations, civic organization, etc. will enjoy "buying" your gift (donating)! It is up to you to take the time and effort to make your charity a gift with a big gold bow that is worth their attention, when so many other charities are vying for the same dollars! Best wishes for making your charity the perfect package with the gold bow of passion on top for increased fundraising dollars!

Wish Five

Wishing for Vivacious Volunteers!

   The number one way to recruit more volunteers is to learn more about them by BEING one! The very first time I volunteered was for "Dress for Success." It was in the basement of another charity, and I was feeling a little apprehensive. This would be the first time that I would be face-to-face with women prisoners. If you are not familiar with the charity, they provide gently used interview apparel to women just getting out of prison or women that are entering the workforce and cannot afford appropriate clothing (I am not an official spokeswoman for them and this is my personal understanding of their organization). I asked one of the workers how I could tell, if the woman was a prisoner. I guess that I had watched too much television and thought they would pull a "shank" on me. She told me to look for a certain address and probably thought this was amusing. We have to understand that volunteers can be apprehensive in new situations with perceived or even real danger.

The first woman came walking down the stairs and the first thing I saw was a pair of black, ugly "men" shoes. My first thought was "prisoner". Being a shoe connoisseur, I know NO woman would wear these shoes by choice. The woman's name was Mary, and she looked like "the life had been sucked out of her." Her head was bowed and shoulders were slumped. I said a quick hello and took her shopping in the makeshift store. We found her a beautiful yellow suit and added an orange blouse that was stunning against her rich chocolate skin and hair. We added a scarf with swirls of these colors on a white background and, of course, found her some wonderful shoes with a purse. She walked out to the mirror no longer like a worn woman, but more like a confident warrior ready to take on the world. She changed my life. Wow! What a transformation a few clothes and a little friendship can make. Footnote: I always tell teenage girls in my seminars, "You never want to go to prison, because they make you wear ugly shoes." LOL

You may say, "Jeanette, that was a lovely story, but what does this have to do with helping me recruit and retain volunteers?" The rest of this story is that I had previously worked for the Finishing Director for the Miss Oklahoma Pageant. I had been a color consultant and make-up artist, attended and even taught a few wardrobe classes. I love doing makeovers. I hate garage sales! I hate sorting and organizing used, smelly clothing, however there were volunteers that absolutely love opening bags of donated clothing and searching for treasures. These workers allowed me to do what I truly enjoyed. I looked forward to returning to help other women with their interview wardrobe and lifting their spirits.

It is vital to find out what your volunteers like to do, and let them pick their job. If you assign them to a task that needs to be done (like cleaning your bathroom), they will hate it and you will lose them. If you take the time as a leader to do every volunteer task, you will grow to appreciate your volunteers more. This is suggested in many business books to do an occasional "ride along" in order to understand the workers' questions and concerns about a job. It will also help to understand the realistic demands and time a job should take. Take time to walk in their shoes or change their shoes to prettier ones. You know what I mean!

Personal stories are probably the best, because I can tell you how I felt as a volunteer. I had taken some time off for personal reasons and was trying to decide my next move in life. There is this wonderful large charity that assists the poor with a full service grocery story, medical and dental clinic, housing, utilities, legal, etc. This organization has been around for about 30 years and in this new location for a year. They wanted to celebrate their one year anniversary and raise community awareness for additional volunteers and funding. They had previously held an event called "NeighborFest", A Celebration of Unity. This would be my volunteer job for almost six months as the Chairwoman for this annual undertaking. I love putting on special events and this one was equivalent to a big party for 700.

This charity was located in an impoverished area that is in the news almost daily, reporting another shooting or crime. Two wonderful foundations had purchased an abandoned, 125,000 square feet strip mall to house this charity. This charity's section took up 40,000 feet and the rest could be rented to fund their charity long-term. These facts and figures are to the best of my knowledge. What I am trying to say is that this is a massive and wonderful charity in an area that truly needs it.

This required an effort of about 700 volunteer hours on my part, and I was partnered with two disgruntled employees. Ouch! One had marketed in this community through her church and this charity. She really taught me the dos and don'ts about her community. This area was closely connected through their churches and the Bishops and First Ladies that oversaw them. She was mostly involved in her church of about 700 and that was her networking source.

The other woman had been with this charity for many, many years. This woman appeared very sweet in front of others and argued with me on every issue of this event. Professional printing for this event could have been done very cost effectively, but this was "her" job. It took her months to complete simple projects and she used many, many expensive color cartridges. This is a prime example about how it is cheaper many times to hire a professional to do a job right, and it saves money in the long run. Most companies will give large discounts for being a 501c3 charity. If you offer to pay, but take the time to explain the importance of your service to their community, they may just donate it for free. This works. They really enjoy giving what they have to give instead of being asked for money. I have made many friends this way and received thousands of dollars of donated items. PS. They especially enjoy the surprise plaque that I bring to their business for display with their name displayed boldly and my charity's logo proudly added. This also serves as a way to create awareness for your charity to their customers. Their customers usually like the idea of giving their business to companies that contribute to the community. This will be discussed in detail in the barter section.

This was one of the most challenging events of my life. It was in a culture that I did not understand and had not previously networked. I caught myself helping out in every area, because they were usually shorthanded with volunteers. I learned an immense amount about how to run a charity. This was not the official reason that I was there or at least that is what I thought. NFN is referred to the "University of Poverty." I also had the rare opportunity to work with another volunteer that contributed greatly to my personal and spiritual growth and knowledge. This again was not the reason that I was there, or so I thought, only to learn later that the connections that I had made and the lessons that I had learned were exactly what I needed to be the Executive of a future charity.

Anyway, the day arrived and so did the media. For once this area received good press. We had invited every mayor, Chamber of Commerce leader, politician, and community leader from the region to attend in order for them to understand the services that were available to every one of their citizens in need. This was the only free dental clinic in the state at the time, I believe. Rain was in the forecast and all you event planners know that this is not good for an outdoor event. I will never forget standing in the parking lot with every vendor in place and watching and listening as the parade came over the hill toward the entrance of the center. There were not streets lined with a crowd, but the clouds parted and the sun shone and a police truck with lights flashing appeared. The crowd was all following the cars that led the possession with Mayor Bill LaFortune riding in the lead car as the Grand Marshall. He had been so very kind to proclaim this day on June 4, 2005 as "Day of Unity" in the City. A couple of State Representatives and the Bishop and First Lady were following in convertibles. There were a plethora of groups from the community and even nuns on motorcycles. This attracted the media as an unusual display of unity. The irony of this was that the priest who started this charity about thirty years ago left the priesthood to begin this charity and was known as a rebel. He would help parishioners with car repairs and give people food or whatever they needed. If it had not have been for the employee that invited her church to attend, (with over 500 showing up), our parade and festival would have been a bust. If it had not have been for the business and group connections of the other employee, our parade or vendor booths would not have been filled. I was able to cast the vision for this event to be as big and bold as possible. My job was to incorporate all of my charity, business, and media connections that I possessed. My job was to build goodwill in the area. Although many did not attend, they were able to read about this effort for unity in the region and watch it on the nightly local news reporting good news for a change.

I was burned out after this event, but it was time for me to go. I had learned my lessons and networked with a whole new group of people. I had enjoyed my time and felt happy and frustrated most of the time. One of the biggest lessons that I learned was that, as a volunteer, you have to be able to not only cast the vision, but have the freedom to carry out the vision for success. It is discouraging to be discounted by others, because you are not getting paid or they think that you want their job. My advice is to love and appreciate your volunteers. Give them a title of respect and the freedom to do what they do best, but remember don't give an accountant an event planning job and definitely don't give an event planner an accounting job. Ask your volunteers what they want to do and help them do it. Don't micromanage! Spend the time up front to get to know them as a person. Explain the job and your expectations, kindly. Never treat them like an hourly employee and make them explain why they did not show up. Ask them kindly to call, if they have something they need to do, or if they just want to go to one of their children's school plays. Be kind and understanding. They are saving you money! You are not paying them, and most likely you cannot afford to do so.

Six month of approximately 700 hours of my time, at a minimum of $25 an hour equals $17,500 plus I *incurred* and paid $4,000 of expenses. There is monetary value for every volunteer. I remember a couple that volunteers for a living since they have retired. They rock the babies at the hospital on Monday, help out at the church on Tuesdays, drive for Meals-On-Wheels on Wednesdays, you get the picture. They were getting ready to quit the charity for which I was the ED. I had heard about all the hours that they had donated to this charity. I scheduled an appointment with them to hear their concerns about why they were getting ready to quit. I had just walked in the door and needed them extremely. There were very few volunteers due to the poor treatment of past ones. Her frustration was that she truly cared for people, and her husband cared dearly for her and helped her with all her endeavors. These are smart people that came from management in an oil company. They understood business and the importance of getting the job done. They understood professionalism and timing. This goes back to when you hire professionals, don't tell them how to do their job and give them the freedom to do it. We had a sign in the office for a while that said, "What Kayla wants Kayla gets!" I put it there. I appreciated the 200 plus hours *per month* that she and Mitch volunteered, and I told them often. I bought their lunch out of the organization kitty and never apologized for it. I made sure we celebrated her birthday by taking them out to lunch with a gift in hand. Our charity could not afford these volunteers, but we could buy a lunch for them and give them a plaque in appreciation. We also could sing their praises in print and media to let them and their friends know about all of their good works. They never asked, but she often said how much she appreciated being thanked.

The board never took the time to personally thank her, and this couple had volunteered for probably four or five years. The board fired her when one of their feelings was hurt. Boards need to appreciate and thank their volunteers and employees. I'm sure most charitable employees are overworked and underpaid for their services. Boards are volunteers, also. They too need to be loved and appreciated. We will talk later about Board Members, if you want to rant and rave a little later, that will be OK!

As I always try to do when going into a new and usually bad situation, I start out, "Hi, my name is Jeanette North, let's start over. How can I help you or what do you need?" New management can address poor past relationships in an organization and build stronger new relationships, if handled correctly. I had seen many times that these strained relationships are disregarded completely, when they need to be addressed and mended. Marketing experts always say it is cheaper to keep a customer; in this case a volunteer, instead of finding new ones. Spend time up front to repair broken bridges and find out what the volunteers need and want. It probably is the same thing you would need and want, if you walked in their shoes. Don't assume, ask, but most of all listen, and they will tell you.

I just wanted a plaque to document and award my hard work. I have purchased beautiful plaques for about $10 to $14 each. If it even cost your organization $20 and about 30 minutes to design a specialized and individualized one for $21,500 worth of service and donation, I don't care who you are, that is a wonderful profit margin in any book. Find out what they want and give it to them. I did not want a pizza party with a paper generic certificate in exchange for $21,500 worth of work. I wanted an inexpensive plaque to commemorate my service with this charity. Ask what a volunteer wants, don't assume!

While we are on this subject, no one owes you anything. Charities are notorious for discounting the goods and services donated to their charities by giving and loving souls. Many do not even take the time to say "thank you!" They expect that people are there to be worked to the bone, treated like slaves, and sent on their way until the next time they are ready to USE them. Say "thank you" often. Starbucks donated lovely coffee mugs and other gifts that had been discontinued. I put these aside for our volunteers and made sure to tell Starbucks how much we enjoyed being able to give these to volunteers. They also donated day old pastries and we were able to "treat" our volunteers regularly. Have a fresh pot of coffee and a small fridge of various soft drinks and water for your volunteers, but you say that this cost money that the charity could use. If I can give a $5 sandwich, bag of chips and a drink to a volunteer that has done three months of bookkeeping, filing, organizing, sorting, etc., it is a lot less than hiring an employee with benefits to do these jobs. Let's say a day's work would cost you $100 and you spent $8 on lunch, your charity just made $92. You may say, Jeanette, this is so very elementary. Well, it may be, but you will not believe the charities that do not see this value. I just wanted to put it out there in black and white. This is why I read, so I can be reminded of things I already know and remember to appreciate them. In this case, it's the value of volunteers.

Volunteerism *is* more than helping the charity most of the time; it is the one volunteering that *reaps the* benefits from the experience. One great recruitment hint is to look for ladies of means without meaning in their lives. These are the woman trying to find happiness in the shopping mall or the "Prozac Princesses" as I *lovingly* call them. These are volunteers that need your organization to help them find their purpose in life that they so desperately need. They are mostly well connected to money people and love to plan and host parties. With the right social finesse, these women will empower your organizations in ways you will never believe. We will talk more about these ladies, who will make wonderful volunteers as "Gala Gals" for your next big fundraiser.

Your job as a leader of the organization is to work with a volunteer coordinator (this is a must) and to motivate your choice workers. Volunteers are workers who choose to work. Let them know that they are making a difference in their community or wherever help is being received. The most fun evening that I can remember was the first year we did a "Cookies and Milk with Santa" for our children. Each client and their children came to a party with Santa and received a small wood toy, milled by a group of woodworkers. There were cookies, milk and juice provided by a very supportive hospital. In another room was an additional Santa who was a board member for our Spanish speaking children. There were volunteers taking Santa pictures with the children for the parents. There were volunteers that had worked tirelessly creating games and crafts for the children. One volunteer had to quit her job due to stress. She showed up daily for about two months and even walked to work in an ice storm, because she could not get her car out of her garage. She will always be remembered as one of the most dedicated volunteers ever. We cried when her husband took a job out of state.

This event had been planned for months. Large three foot stockings were filled by local families and business for our children in need. These were purchased at the local dollar store. There were volunteers that signed families up, helped with their wish list, shopped for them, received presents, kept them accurate, on and on. For this particular one, the National Honor Society and local high school football boys even provided valet service for parents to drive-thru to receive a Holiday meal complete with a turkey or ham. The children's gifts were hidden in large black trash bags. There was an additional group of volunteers that provided assembling for bicycles and made special arrangements for pick-up. We used clipboards for volunteers to sign-in and out, and there were probably over 300 not including all the families that picked-up a wish list, shopped, and delivered to our door. The second year we adjusted the process and were able to provide Christmas gifts to over 600 children and disabled adults. We had most of these volunteers return from our Back-to-School supply project and Thanksgiving Basket project. I believe that communities are starving for local projects to make a difference. We as charities are great to basically say, "Give us your money and get out of our way!" I know we don't say that literally, but we say it with our actions. People will give their time and/or money, if they can see results of their actions. They are sick and tired of all the abuse and misuse of funds with little results. Showing due diligence of funds and numbers of people served will attract volunteers to your organization like mosquitoes to perfumed skin. We experienced turning volunteers away and rescheduling them for other times. Remember Kayla, she was the master organizer of all of these events, and I just *had* to go out and network for whatever goods and services that we needed.

Treat volunteers like you would want to be treated as a volunteer. Oh! You haven't volunteered, yet. Do it! Do it now! When you have a project, determine the number of volunteers needed and the age of volunteers that could successfully complete the task. We worked closely with the Boy and Girl Scouts, women and civic groups, don't forget the sports teams and retirement centers. Did you know that Starbucks, Best Buy and many other corporations encourage volunteerism and even give grants for their efforts? Remember to matchup the groups to the projects. Most of all, when someone walks into your charity, listen to their needs and desires to help your organization. Take action to get them started today or tomorrow, before the mood passes! They may just be the one that walks to work in an ice storm to volunteer. Best wishes for more vivacious volunteers!

Note the number one change you want to make in this area. _____

_____
_____
_____
_____
_____
_____
_____
_____
_____
_____
_____

Wish Six

Wishing for Powerful Presentations!

"They don't care how much you know, until they know how much you care" is an old saying that still rings true. The purpose of this chapter is to provide a simple three step approach for creating presentations with passion including some "real life" examples. The key element to giving a great presentation is **passion!** Whether at a gala or on the steps of a capitol building, presentation success depends on a simple three step approach: Love your subject! Love your audience! Love the opportunity to make a difference!

The first three great orators of passion that come to mind are John F. Kennedy, Martin Luther King, and Abraham Lincoln. According to Webster's New World Dictionary (Agnes, Laird and Staff), passion is any emotion, as hate, love, fear, etc., intense emotional excitement, as rage, enthusiasm, lust, etc., or the object of any strong desire. Kennedy spoke with passion about duty to country in his January 20, 1961, Inaugural speech: "Ask not what your country can do for you" (Famous Quotes). Martin Luther King stirred a nation with his speech: "I Have a Dream" (Wikipedia). He made a difference through his strong belief in civil rights and rallied others to action!

Abraham Lincoln spoke from the back of a train for just over two minutes to deliver his Gettysburg Address. "Four score and seven years ago, our fathers brought forth on this continent…that all men are created equal (Wikipedia)." Recently, I caught a glimpse of an episode about Lincoln on the History Channel (The History Channel). He was ill with a slight case of smallpox when he delivered this short speech. The previous speaker spoke for over two hours. It was said that he referred to this speech as going over like a "wet blanket!" The people were so very quiet afterwards. He did not realize; He had just given a speech that would long be remembered. There is no doubt that these men loved their subject matter. It showed in their passion and we still remember!

The first step is to love your subject (mission), and a great way to investigate a message for presentation is to learn from experts. Learn techniques from the classic orators mentioned above or seek out modern day speakers as mentors. A mentor is a person who acts as a guide, trainer, coach, and counselor; who teaches you the informal rules of an organization or a field; and who imparts the kinds of wisdom that come from firsthand experience (Adler and Elmhorst). Let's explore three modern day speakers that teach about the power of the message for presentation.

In October 2000, Jim Stovall became my mentor. He wrote "The Ultimate Gift" (The Ultimate Gift) and produced the movie. His credentials are numerous, therefore to learn more him, visit www.jimstovall.com (Stovall, Jim Stovall). He speaks to over a million people a year and has even spoken in Madison Square Garden. Oh! Did I mention that he achieved all of this success after he became blind? Once, I asked him about making a particular decision and his sage advice was, "If you only had a year to live, what would you do?" (Stovall, President, Narrative Television Network). Speeches must be planned with this kind of passion for your message; as if this may be the last speech you will ever give.

Anthony Robbins is one of the greatest modern day motivational speakers. He has a series of audio tapes called: Personal Power! A 30-Day Program for Unlimited Success (Tony Robbins). In this series he says, "I don't say this to impress you, but to impress upon you!" This is sage advice when delivering a message. He even goes on to say that it is not how eloquent he speaks, but the importance of the message about making good decisions. He displays outrageous enthusiasm and passion for his message with the tagline of "Program yourself for total success." If you want to see passion in a message, watch one of his presentations.

The third speaker, you must hear about, is my friend Billy Robbins-no relation to Tony. I met him through the National Speakers Association of Oklahoma (National Speakers Association of Oklahoma) as an apprentice. It is one of the best organizations in the nation for individuals seeking to enter this field. He has real passion when it comes to his message of safety in the workplace. His website and subject matter is: www.hookedonsafety.com (Hooked on Safety). You see, he lost both of his arms from the elbows down and wears hooks for hands. An accident from being electrocuted in the workplace caused his "disability". He lived, that was a miracle! Billy became very wealthy from telling his story.

It is the passion of the message that created success for these modern day speakers and it will create successful presentations for you.

Love your audience is the second easy step for presentation success. My friend GiGi pretends that she is having a good cup of tea with a friend. This is her technique for a calm relaxed presentation. Finding a person in the audience with a very friendly face and supportive smile is my recommendation. A lady in a red dress was sitting in the middle of the room shaking her head "yes" during my first paid speech. This gave me the confidence to connect with my audience and continue my message.

Audience background and anticipated reaction influence your vocabulary and the way you organize and present the information (Brantley and Miller). While working for a large utility company as a marketing representative, I chose to give a sales promotion to 200 striking power plant workers. No one from the corporate office had spoken to this group for about two years, since the strike. This was the exact reason that we should go. After serving trays of the largest and best cookies in town, many bags of candy, including lemonade and other drinks on a very hot day, the audience laughed and smiled before this meeting. It was in part of a union hall meeting and mostly men. This would be considered a hostile environment in almost any textbook. The audience was polite, but barely receptive to my "corporate" message. At the close, I remember a very large man wearing overalls and a bandana walking away and his pockets bulged with candy. There is an old saying in the speaking field: "If you help just one person that day, you did your job." I knew that I had made a difference in this man's life that day and in the relations between these two groups.

It does not matter who is in your audience. If you love them and deliver a passionate message, they will respond. Before returning to college, I was the Executive Director of a charity. Part of my duties was to raise money through special events. This included two extravagant galas and a dinner party with over 175 being the smallest to almost 400 audience members and dignitaries. While on stage, I looked around to see a State Senator, State Representative, two Mayors, County Commissioner, hospital administrator, physicians, bank presidents, etc. With an Associate Degree and no formal speech training, what was I doing there? I knew more about the needs of the poor in our community than they knew. I knew they cared and had the means to donate the necessary funds. The results of loving these three audiences raised over $144,000 for our charity!

An audience can be a troop of scouts in a parking lot to a black tie affair including the dignitaries mentioned above. Love your audience by showing respect for them through preparation, organization, eye contact, visual aids, having fun (Irwin) and above all honesty from your heart. Show respect for them through your efforts to present yourself and all of your materials professionally. Don't waste their time. After listening to a former Governor at the end of the speech, I was puzzled. There was no message. He had a wealth of information to share with his audience, but had just focused on himself with no regard for the crowd. I expected more.

Don't worry about stumbling over your words. Years ago, while watching one of the major network morning shows, a newscaster totally messed up the wording of a script. This was during the time she was in salary negotiations as one of the highest paid women in television. Professionals, who are paid millions even falter, it is a human characteristic.

An unknown college student was worrying about getting up in front of a class. I suggested that she tell the audience about her Harley motorcycle rides with her boyfriend including all the equipment necessary for safety and style, of course. I enjoyed listening to her stories about their weekend rides and all the steps to get ready for them. She then focused on her love for Harleys and her message to the audience. The nerves disappeared and she did a fantastic presentation. Whether you are an audience member or the presenter, show love for the message and for all the participants during the interaction time. The result will be more than a presentation. It could be a life changing event for almost everyone present!

The third and final step is to love the opportunity to make a difference. In a seminar years ago, I still remember the presenter referring to this example. Like an Olympic champion, it is necessary to "stick the landing!" In gymnastics this expression is used to explain the conclusion of a performance. A second example in the speaking field is a "golden nugget." This is the unforgettable knowledge. Did you leave the audience with at least one piece of knowledge that they can carry with them?

A Jewish woman who survived the Holocaust was the speaker at a luncheon for a very prestigious ladies networking group. She usually only spoke to elementary children, but made an exception for a friend and member. She was very reserved and told us that she was NOT a speaker. When her story began, she was a ten year old girl walking through a line where children were separated from their parents. The children were killed. The person making these decisions let her go through with her mom and grandmother. You could have "heard a feather drop" as the saying goes. She continued her story about the pain and hunger. They were fed potato skins as the staple of their diet. She closed by telling all of her life lessons taken from this experience. She told us to always remember to eat your potato skins! She believed that these peels were one of the main reasons she lived to tell this story. To this day, I can NOT eat a potato skin without thinking about this lovely Jewish woman and how blessed my life has been! She took the opportunity to speak to our group and leave us a "golden nugget." She made a difference in my life by reminding me to count my blessings.

Every speaker longs to know what it would be like to receive a standing ovation for their message. I have received only one, and it was the most humbling experience of my life. I felt the desire to give my largest donation to date to the local Rotary Club for their Nicaraguan Water Well Project. The purpose of this gift was to encourage others to donate to this most worthy project.

While watching Rhett, my little grandson, play in the bath one day, I realized that he would probably never experience the lack of water. As I walked by the pool with 10,000 gallons of water, I thought about how very blessed Americans are to have an abundance of this resource. A compelling presentation about this project through Rotary made me think about the children without water or only contaminated water in villages in Nicaragua.

In a very short impromptu speech, I challenged these business leaders to help Nicaraguan children by funding water wells in honor of their grandchildren. I credit the power of the message for this peer audience response. They donated a second well last year during their first year to participate in this program. My grandson's love for water encouraged me to give and then encourage others. What a rare opportunity, it was, to visit Nicaragua and see the difference water makes!

Presentations are more than the structure of a title page, outline, body with an introduction, body, conclusion, etc. (Brantley and Miller). They are about a message with a purpose and usually in a story-telling format. They don't need to be complicated to leave an impact. Think about the short but classic speeches by King or Lincoln. Emulate the style of the famous modern day great speakers like Jim Stovall, Tony Robbins, to the lesser known ones as Billy Robbins. Did your audience receive their golden nugget of knowledge for their time?

There are many, many books about presentations. Two that I would recommend for additional information are: <u>Speak and Grow Rich by Dottie Walters and Lilly Walters </u>(Walters and Walters) and<u> 7 Steps to Fearless Speaking by Lilyan Wilder </u>(Wilder). Use these three simple little steps to give presentations with passion:

Love your subject! Love your audience! Love the opportunity to make a difference!

"Jeanette, I'm trying to learn how to raise money for my charity and you are giving me a textbook lesson about how to give a speech, why?" I'll answer with a story, who could have guessed? This most wonderful woman ran a most worthy charity, but almost refused to have her picture taken for the society section of a large newspaper to promote a seminar that I was hosting for them. I understand shyness, humility, etc. but the first rule of marketing is: Let them know who you are and what you do. You must become known as the Charity Lady or Man in your community or the (insert the name of your charity) Lady or Man. The best way to achieve this is to attend every chamber of commerce meeting, civic organization, ladies group, or any other open meeting in your coverage area. Get to know the members and what their mission or purpose is. Then try to book a time for a presentation about your mission.

Our local Rotary was one of these groups that I targeted as a new ED. I attended a few meetings and told them who I was and what charity that I worked for. You could feel the cool breeze and I began to ask a few friendly faces what the problem was between these two organizations. There had been various ED's and the organization was sloppy and unorganized and did not always live up to their commitments. In about three or four months, I was called in when a speaker could not attend. I remember feeling that cool breeze again and seeing many of the mostly male audience with their arms folded over their chests. This is a fairly common sign of a barrier between the audience member and the speaker or message of the speaker. This was a rather intimidating situation similar to the time at the power plant. I remember thinking, "Just get out the first few words and you have your note card to remind you of each program. Add a short little story to give it meaning about why they should support and give to their charity." After all, our charity took care of their citizens in need. My tag line was: "O-ville citizens helping O-ville citizens in need and Collinsville, too!" Remember, if you don't remember anything else in the book, "Let them know who you are and what you do!" Well, remember two things and the other is your "elevator speech." (Wikipedia)

An **elevator pitch** is an overview of an idea for a product, service, or project. The name reflects the fact that an elevator pitch can be delivered in the time span of an elevator ride (for example, thirty seconds and 100-150 words).

"Hi, I'm Jeanette North, the new Executive Director of OCR." I went on to tell of all the new and exciting events happening at our agency with personal stories of interaction with clients. The audience was the father figures of the community including the school superintendent, bank presidents, and others of influence and donation possibilities. I perceived this group as the most influential in our city. Over the next 22 months, I spoke with our Rotary many, many times and promoted every event and program of our charity on a regular basis. We received regular annual donations including a yearly 6 am shopping spree with these same, mostly men, buying Christmas gifts for local children and disabled adults in need. This was a most enjoyable experience, and it received favorable press for both organizations. We were their local charity of choice including donations from many of their members' businesses. Their mission became one of my personal favorites and a place for my donations. In the end, I was given the "Service Above Self"

Award and became an honorary Rotarian with this fantastic group of friends still to this day.

Did you catch my donations went to another charity? I believe, if you sow your personal seeds of giving into another charity, your charity will be blessed. Case in point is while I was sitting in a weekly Rotary meeting my phone rang. I know this is rude, but I thought for sure that I had turned it off. I quickly disconnected the call and it rang again. This was during a presentation of all the wonderful work that this organization does worldwide. A regional representative told of the Nicaraguan Water Well Project and I thought, "Yes, I gave to that!" He continued the slide presentation and told of the Wheelchair Project and I thought, "Yes, I gave to that!" The phone rang. It was a foundation to say that we had received the full amount of $50,000 for our counseling project. Yes, I believe that one of the best ways to raise funds for your charity is to give your personal donations to other charities. If you give to your own charity, you are just padding your fundraising numbers, but it is ok to buy a table at your gala, and I believe that you should. Presentations are a must to raise the money necessary to fulfill your mission goals, but they must show evidence of: Love your subject! Love your audience! Love the opportunity to make a difference! Best wishes for more powerful presentations!

Notes:_____

_____

_____

_____

_____

_____

_____

_____

Wish Seven

Wishing for a Political Pelican!

There is an old saying that "You can't fight city hall!" This chapter is based on a true story that tells of one community's struggle to provide public transportation especially for their elderly, disabled and poor and the unexpected political resistance. It was very common for our charity to receive daily requests for transportation from the elderly or poor. Our city did not have a taxi service and the local churches and our charity tried to fulfill these needs. Transportation was a big problem without a quick or easy solution.

Transportation was part of our mission, but very few volunteers wanted the legal and insurance liability. A little old lady in a wheelchair called and just wanted a ride to the beauty shop. A blind, widowed woman needed a ride to her doctor's office. The calls just poured in and our charity made an effort to meet each need. Within two weeks, we had become the local taxi service for our citizens in need. What could be done?

C-more, a city close to the size of our city, had a public transportation service called Pelivan Transit. This organization was named after the pelicans that migrate to Grand Lake every year. After making four calls, Debbie McGlasson, the Director, explained this wonderful service (McGlasson). Pelivan offers transportation to workplaces, doctor's offices, grocery stores and appointments for a small fee (Plummer, O-ville explores options for public transportation). She made a few phone calls and found that O-ville was on the borderline to receive this "rural" service. She could "piggyback" our grant request with other cities, but had to complete a public notice and meeting including letters of support. Her concern was the Federal grant deadline was only a month away!

An article headline O-ville Explores Options for Public Transportation was in the *Tulsa World* on April 24, 2007 (Plummer, O-ville explores options for public transportation). This documented the first Public Meeting held by Grand Gateway Economic Development Association, the non-profit operators of Pelivan Transit. It was attended by a consortium of local business leaders including representation from two hospitals, churches, city, banks, non-profits and the director of Oklahoma's largest retirement village. This was a perfect example of ethics of care, which is an ethic that emphasizes caring for the concrete well being of those near to us (Velasquez). This group was investigating the possibilities of public transportation for their local citizens, clients and customers in need.

In the *O-ville Reporter* on June 25, 2007, a headline read: $120,000 Grant Awarded for O-ville Transit Service (Staff). There were only three new grants given in the state of Oklahoma and O-ville received the largest. The cost to provide two six-passenger ADA mini vans would be $66,200 with grant funding for $54,946. The local match required would be $11,254. Fares for those under 60 would be $2 one way in the city and $3 for rural routes, two miles outside city limits. For those over 60 the cost could be $1.75 one way no matter the rider's age (Staff). Grand Gateway operates the program including dispatcher, drivers, gas, insurance and all other aspects of operation. The Federal Government would match approximately 80% of the cost of new vehicles and 50% of the administration.

The title of the article City of O-ville, Pelivan Transit: Officials Debate Public Transportation Grant by Sara Plummer was in the *Tulsa World*, World Staff Writer (Plummer, City of O-ville, Pelivan Transit: Officials debate public transportation grant). She documented a meeting held on June 27th. This meeting for Stage two was held at a foundation in the Bailey Medical Center, O-ville, Oklahoma. The purpose was to discuss how and when this program would be implemented and the sources of match funds with Debbie McGlasson, the Director of Pelivan Transit. This service would be scheduled to begin on October 1, 2007 (Plummer, City of O-ville, Pelivan Transit: Officials debate public transportation grant). The consortium needed to proceed quickly in order to provide this most valuable service to their elderly and poor. Since Pelivan Transit had always contracted for their services with cities, it was deemed necessary for the City of O-ville to enter into this contract. This was on the advice of a hospital administrator and bank president. The consortium would have to form an organization to enter into this contract and there was not enough time. The city would have to match funding on a yearly basis to provide stability and continue this service's availability to their citizens.

The problem was that a few city officials were mad. They had tried to provide transportation for the last five years! This transportation solution was not their idea and the media was not going to give them credit for it. It was more desirable for them to ban this service for personal ego reasons than to accommodate their citizens' transportation needs. According to <u>Business Ethics Concepts and Cases</u>, this is a textbook example of the approaches to the ethics of political tactics in respect to utilitarian (Velasquez). It was NOT these city officials' intent to advance this socially beneficial program. This consortium of concerned citizens with the assistance of the Pelivan Director had secured the majority of funding. The city could not do in 5 years what this group did in five month with the God's help.

Debbie McGlasson met with this small group of city officials about the September 11th City Council workshop. She was told not to attend that "they" would take care of this issue. This meeting set the agenda for the upcoming City Council meeting on September 18th. This determined small group of city officials wanted to keep Pelivan off the agenda the following week in this "closed" workshop. Citizens could attend, but could not speak. This was difficult with the lies circulating about the absorbent future cost of this service. The purpose was to push Pelivan to the October meeting, after the grant money match had expired. This would cancel this project and look in the public's eye as though this unscrupulous group really tried to make it work.

The underlying goal of this small group was to make the City Council believe that this service would cost over $177,000 the following year, and it was not a good deal for the city. I personally found out about this move and secured the documentation from the Director with the "true" facts from Pelivan Transit (McGlasson). The projection was that it would cost the city about $40,000 the first year and $50,000 the second year and vary slightly depending on the number of vans added. The figures were based on other cities of similar size. In a whistle blowing effort to expose these untrue accusations, this documentation was mailed directly to each councilor's home. The truth was: For the price of one luxury car, our community could benefit from public transportation for this year.

During this exhausting fight with city hall to bring transportation to our community, my husband and I decided to find solitude at our small beach condo in Corpus Christie. This is our safe place to revitalize and renew our spirits, when life gets a little too hectic. We had broken up the 10 and a half hour drive into two days, which was unusual for us. It was midday and as I walked down the narrow hallway, it felt so calm and restful. Heading directly to the roman shades, I seemed to pull them up and open the door almost simultaneously. Straight to our deck overlooking the ocean, there on the shoreline were over 20 pelicans lined up about a foot apart and seemed ready for orders to takeoff. They stay there long enough for me to count them twice. This was very unusual, because it is more common to see only two or three together. I remember tears came to my eyes, because I knew this was a sign from God that this project was a done deal. I never worried again about who would win this fight, but I never quit working on it until the final vote was cast. The battle continued on.

One city official was also, on the board of the charity where I worked. The night before the City Council meeting, he "hijacked" our monthly board meeting. He announced that there would be a vote on Pelivan the following evening. As a city official, he explained his view for all the reasons that this was not a good idea for our community. He never mentioned that transportation was part of the mission of this charity. It was in the bylaws that board members would support the mission.

A public notice email was circulated about the City Council meeting on September 18th to church members, charity volunteers, and many other groups. It encouraged citizens to attend and support this transportation service. A petition was also circulated and over 200 names were gathered in about a 24 hour period in support of this service. The political counter move was leading citizens to believe on the city's website that the city was 100% behind this issue. Since it had been very public about the large amount of potential grant money to be received, there would be no reason for concerned citizens to attend this meeting. This effort was to block public attendance and attention to this issue.

September 18th arrived. It felt like a "showdown at OK Corral" as the saying goes! The old church that now houses the City Council meetings was full. Debbie McGlasson was not there at the city's request. One of the city representatives delivered the Pelivan issue from his point of view. Other city officials paraded to the podium with their rehearsed view of why this was not a good idea. This match money could pay for one more police or fireman to keep our city safe. This argument has already surfaced. This amount for $41,975 was not included in this year's budget, but this Federal and State grant money of $188,755 was unexpected. It was like watching a good ping pong match. Good versus evil. Truth versus lies; Politicians versus citizens; Argument verses argument. Any citizen could speak for three minutes, if they requested their time before the meeting. This was my speech and release made available to the media:

PRESS RELEASE

City Council Meeting

September 18, 2007 6:30pm

Pelivan Transit

Honorable Mayor Steve, Susan, Doug, DJ and new member Joe, hello, I'm Jeanette North, Executive Director of O-ville Community Resources. Did you know that the City has received almost $10,000 from OCR since June 2006 to help our poor keep their water and city utilities on? We provided 865 students at risk in O-ville Public Schools with grade-appropriate school supplies just this school year and 150 local families with Thanksgiving meals and 430 children and 6 disabled adults with Christmas gifts in 2006 with the help of Rotary, Boy Scouts, Churches and other local organizations. **Transportation** is part of our mission, also.

Tonight, Debbie McGlasson brings us $188,755 that has been allocated to our O-ville community. There were only three of these Federal grants given in the state of Oklahoma this year and O-ville received the largest for over $150,000. Debbie also secured another grant for state funding for over $37,000. For every dollar the Council invests we will receive over $4.60 in return. For the price of one luxury car ($41,975), we can receive this money.

If you say this money could be spent better to improve roads, **BUT** we have roads. If you say, it could be spent better to provide more police or firemen, **BUT** we do have policemen and firemen. O-ville **does not** have any form of public transportation to provide for our citizens. NOW, IS THE BEST TIME TO INVESTMENT IN this "golden opportunity" in 2007!

Have you ever seen a stack of million dollar bills, this is almost 1/5 of that pile of money sitting before you. When you receive grant money, this money is taken from other worthy projects, therefore if you return this money; it is a slim to null chance that O-ville would ever receive it again. Tonight it is: will you trade the price of one car $41,975 to receive

$188,755. This is a onetime… **DEAL OR NO DEAL!**

In closing, O-ville advertises on billboards and in television commercials that O-ville is the "City of Character." Some of the character traits are: (1) benevolence, etc. Character is not just something you talk about; it is something you can show by VOTING **YES.** Tomorrow's headlines could read **City of Character shows character!** By voting **YES** you will provide transportation for O-ville's elderly, disabled, poor and general public.

OR

City of Character lacks character! By voting **NO to providing** public transportation so our elderly can get to their doctor's appointments; **NO** to our disabled citizens to have ADA wheelchair approved transportation, **NO** to our working poor getting to their jobs, when their car breaks down and **NO** to public transportation for our general public.

Your City Council VOTE TONIGHT IS; **YES WE TRULY ARE "THE CITY OF CHARACTER" OR NO IT'S JUST A CAMPAIGN TO MAKE US FEEL GOOD!!!**

On September 19, 2007, Sara Plummer writes in a *Tulsa World* article O-ville City Council: Public Transportation Plan OK'd. "The O-ville City Council voted 3-2 Tuesday to approve city funding for a public transportation program…" was part of the opening line (Plummer, O-ville City Council: Public transportation plan OK'd). Mayor

Cataudella led the discussion in favor of Pelivan Transit. He is very sympathetic to the needs of the poor and elderly. He said, "We talk about quality of life. This is quality of life" (Plummer, O-ville City Council: Public transportation plan OK'd). Councilor Bonebrake believed that it just made good business sense. Jon was the newest member in favor. He followed the Mayor's request for this service, I believe.

On Wednesday, January 30, 2008, the *Tulsa World* headline read: Ticket to Ride, Popularity of Pelivan Transit in O-ville Grows After First Month. According to Eric Wiles, O-ville Community Development Director, "So far, ridership exceeds our expectations. They're doing 12 rides a day a month in. We projected 12 rides a day averaging after a year."(Plummer, Ticket to ride, Popularity of Pelivan Transit in O-ville grows after first month). This article interviewed a lady with cerebral palsy that rides Pelivan to her job.

Her parents were her only transportation source before. Another lady had not be able to drive since a brain aneurism and told how wonderful the service was for her (Plummer, Ticket to ride, Popularity of Pelivan Transit in O-ville grows after first month).

Fast forward to August 21, 2008, the front page headline in the *O-ville Reporter* reads: Council Renews Pelivan Transit's Agreement (Whited). The City Council voted 4-1 in favor of expending of $49,393 to renew this contract. The new agreement runs for a year from October 1, 2008 until September 30, 2009. Eric Wiles told the Council members that ridership was up to 600 a month with two-thirds of the riders being elderly or disabled (Whited).

In conclusion, this victory cost me personally, my position as the Executive Director of the local charity. The board member that was also a city official made sure of this. It was a hard fought battle, but providing transportation to our elderly, disabled and poor was the morally right thing to do. Whistle blowing (Velasquez) to the City Council members was costly, but I would not trade one minute of my former job for this most needed transportation service. Every time, I see one of these vans go by, I thank God for the opportunity to make a difference in the lives of these 600 riders a month.

I distinctly remember telling someone, "I'm not in politics!" He replied, "Oh! Yes you are!" When charities are dealing with social changes in their communities, they are dealing in politics. One State Representative told me to play offense, but don't forget to play defense. He was making the motions of a basketball player being a forward and then a guard. It is a very good idea to seek a few trusted mentors in the political arena in order to better understand how to get things done and whom to trust. This project represented $188,755 of federal and state grants and the $41,975 of city money for a grand total of $230,730 for a partial section of our mission that was never included in our fundraising numbers. It is often better to solve a problem, than to be worried about who get credit for it. Best wishes for finding your political pelican!

Wish Eight

Wishing for a "Queen Bee" of Networking!

The old saying about it's not what you know, it's who you know! This could not be truer when it comes to fundraising. I've always said "Why sell one widget to one person, when you can sell a lot of widgets to a lot of people!" There is only one way you can do that, and that is target the person or company that has the access to those groups of people. Our little company partnered with a large utility company and sold 22 water heaters in one month. Networking is connecting up or as I like to say "Marrying with others success!" I read this somewhere and don't know whom to credit, but I'd like to add a second analogy to it. A popular saying in the corporate world is "getting into bed with someone." The difference in marrying with others is giving exclusive right to one party, associating with their name and being a help mate looking out for their success. The other saying refers to manipulating and using others for your own benefit. One simple network connection can bring in a large donation or a connection to the pipeline that leads to many other potential donors.

The "Queen Bee" technique is taking your message to this flower (organization) and then this flower (donors) and then this flower (media) and another and another. There are times as an ED that you will have the opportunity to introduce a potential donor to another charity, because their mission does not match your mission. I had the opportunity to help a large electronic retail chain give to three other charities after they gave $10,000 to our charity and had to "spread it around." This "Queen Bee" has taken about every individual, corporate, foundation and any other potential donor out for a lunch. This gives you the opportunity to get to know managers, foundation program directors, grant managers, community affairs managers, CEO's, etc. as people. Their family situations, hobbies, company dynamics, etc. are usually like reading a good book, and lunch gives you hopefully an hour to make a personal connection with that person. "I always make friends not business associates that way you have the opportunity to help them and they will help you. It doesn't matter where you land." Some charities don't believe in wasting money on expensive lunches and plaques. I have spent $49 on a networking luncheon with a foundation connection that netted two $5,000 donations and a few smaller ones. I have spent $10 on a plaque to thank a corporation and it encouraged other corporations to donate $1,000 for a table at a gala. In the business world, this makes "cents", but some charities just don't believe in another old saying, "It takes money to make money." I had a very successful bank owner tell me one time, "Never be afraid to spend the money!" He told me of a very expensive piece of property that others would not invest in, but he had the foresight and it paid off in multi millions.

Lunch or coffee are perfect opportunities to network and solidify a connection that can become a long-term friendship and years of profitable networking for your charity. My friend and a bank manager complimented me for just taking the time to come by and visit with her every week or so for "no" reason. She did not mind donating when I asked. My philosophy is you better hang onto your wallets when you see me coming, because I will get into them soon or later! LOL If people know that you are a fundraiser or associated with a 501c3, they expect to be asked for money. They don't even mind giving, if they feel appreciated and thanked. Just don't make them feel pressured or obligated.

Here are 21 "Queen Bee" rules that have served me well.

- ✓ Know who you are working with and "wine and dine" them accordingly.
- ✓ Learn about them from others in your community if possible.
- ✓ Ask them where they would like to eat and have someplace special in mind, if they don't.
- ✓ Clean out your car and dress appropriately.
- ✓ Be on time or call ahead if you are detained.
- ✓ If you are in question as to appropriate table manners, follow their lead.
- ✓ Pick-up the check, if you ask them to lunch. Please note some foundations and politicians can not let you pay for their meals because of policy restrictions. This also includes gifts.
- ✓ Do not ask personal questions about money, etc. Let them offer information.
- ✓ Ask them if they would like dessert. This will give you more time. If you are on a

diet, don't say a word, just order something you don't really like and take small bites. This also gives you the opportunity to sell-sell-sell and they can enjoy their sweets. The same goes for alcohol. Don't announce how you don't drink and everyone who does is a sinner. This is common in our Bible belt section of the country.
- ✓ Keep religious and political views to yourself and steer clear and evasive if questioned.
- ✓ Remember to "close the deal!" Why did you take the time to take them to lunch? Get to know them, before you ask them for a dime, unless this is the only opportunity to ask, therefore be prepared.
- ✓ Be up-front as to why you ask them to lunch. Another old saying "There is no such thing as a free lunch!" If you want them to consider your charity for a future donation,

tell them about all its wonderful attributes and ask them to consider you in their future giving.
- ✓ Don't be pushy or pressure them, because you NEED the money!
- ✓ Don't tell them that your charity only has enough money to last until the end of the month or you might go out of business.
- ✓ Be careful whom you invite to attend. I usually prefer one-on-one contact, but they may want to bring another party from their organization and you might want to bring an additional board member or staff member to equal it out. Prepare the other party as to what goals you need to accomplish in this meeting. Leave all "negative Nellie's" at the office.
- ✓ "Never say anything negative!" This was an unwritten rule in real estate. Show them the big bedroom as you walk past the small

bath. Same with your charity, tell them about all the wonderful programs with a small, sincere story attached. Don't bother them with staff and other internal problems.
- ✓ Tell them how many students you hope to serve with your back-to-school program coming up in two months. Don't waste time promoting a program that was just over. Brag a little on your accomplishments, but emphasize all the upcoming opportunities to give.
- ✓ Enjoy the time and don't answer that cell phone unless it is an emergency! Don't tell them how busy you are and keep looking at your watch or at least where they can see.
- ✓ First, focus on them and their needs and then bring the conversation to your charity and its needs, but most of all make the connection.
- ✓ Give and get a business card before the meeting is over, but it is best to do this up

front, so you don't forget. Email them afterwards and thank them for lunch. This opens your email conversations for future communications. Use the back of their card to make notes of their husband's name, other company contacts, etc. to be used for future reference.

✓ Last of all, if they are a person that is just going to waste your time trying to sell you personal insurance, make-up, etc. and has no interest in helping you with your charity, make a note of this and limit their time to 5 minute phone conversations and no future lunches. Some people have nothing better to do, but waste your time.

The "Queen Bee" takes charge. She oversees the overall production of the honey. When you walk into a crowded room for a meeting make sure you take the time to "buzz" from table to table and meet everyone you don't know and visit quickly with the ones you do know. There was a speaker from a local community college including a foundation. He was almost impossible to contact personally. I "buzzed" up to him and gave him a packet for purchasing a table at our upcoming gala. They purchased one, of course. The President of the college hand delivered my packet to their foundation. Now that is what I call "taking flight!" toward success. Don't sit with the same group at monthly meetings. Make it a point to sit with different individuals or members and follow the same basic rules as taking them to lunch. You are there to work, not just dine.

A good networker will work when they are getting their hair colored, nails polished, or eyebrows waxed. My friend Charles owns the best hair salon in the world as far as I am concerned. They were the former "official hair stylist" for the Miss Oklahoma Pageant. Telling him all about "my" charity and loud enough for others to hear, he happened to mention he was the stylist for the trustee of a major foundation. If we ever decide to build, he would make sure to visit with him and deliver the plans to him. He also has many clients that are "moneyed." Networking is a must for connecting entities that can produce powerful exchanges including large donations.

Remember the number rule of networking is "Let them know who you are and what you do!" Being a person that dresses for my mood, I decided to wear my long pink jacket with a black evening camisole with various colors of bugle beads with a pair of my black slacks. This was for an outing to take my transcript from one college and hand-carry it to another college. Because of the over-the-top outfit for daywear, a man that I believed to be the Dean of the college walked over and introduced himself to me. I explained my reason for being there and took the time to exchange cards. A month later while working with a nonprofit school, it was obvious to me that the classrooms needed for this high school could be provided by the college that serviced mostly adults. There were brand new state-of-the-art empty classrooms available until 4 pm. This was about 30 minutes after the high school would be dismissed. After a 20 minute phone call explaining the potential match and benefits, I set the appointment for the ED and the Dean to meet. I recently learned that this networking resulted in these high school students learning in a college building and being exposed to the possibilities of college. This all happened in three months. This Dean also possessed the power to pick up the phone and find funding for this new affiliation. The short and long term goals of both organizations were to return and keep high school students in school and lift them to their full potential of a college education. Wow! I love networking. It gives synergy to addressing society's problems.

Do you ever work trade shows or festivals? These can be excellent sources of networking for dollars. The key word is work. For a short time, I was a representative for a food vending distributor with a variety of products including Keebler cookies. Our trade show was in a casino and the booth was decorated to reflect the theme. My sequined dealer's vest with white shirt and black pants was the perfect outfit and yes I just went to my closet to get it. I love themes and costumes, because they do attract attention for your product. Not everyone is as flamboyant as this "Queen Bee," therefore be an exaggerated version of yourself or hire a mascot. (The answer is yes, I do have a "Queen Bee" costume!) There were not a lot of participants at this trade show, and most were already my friends and clients. Take this golden opportunity to network with others vendors, especially companies that are noncompetitive. It is a good idea to have an abundance of business cards at all times and updated brochures. Sample food items and candy draw participants like bees to honey. Keep notes on the best potential clients or donors and follow-up on your offer to take them to lunch. You must have a drawing for a themed gift! This will encourage people to give you their names, address, cell number, and email addresses. These will be very useful when finding donors to purchase tickets to your next gala. One friend used a small wooden laundry basket filled with candy, cereal and soda pop from the 50's to attract entries. It was a big hit!

This may just sound like fun to you and a good networker makes it look easy. Running in high heels is the key to networking a room or trade show. Men, high heels may not work as well for you. LOL You will have to continuously think what product would this person buy? What would be the best approach to individual personalities?

Networking is attracting the individuals to your organization that can donate, volunteer, or facilitate your success.

"The Gift of Gab" was given to me at birth. I always said, "If I could find a job that would let me talk and go to lunch, then I would be home!" Sales and marketing is that job, but the real joy of my life was the day that I decided to sell causes instead of widgets. I found my life-long calling to help charities raise money by simply talking to a lot of people and doing what I do best; going to lunch and closing the deal! Best wishes for your exploration of these "Queen Bee" techniques for successful networking!

Notes:_____

_____
_____
_____
_____

<u>Wish Nine</u>

Wishing for a Sales and Marketing Guru!

I can't sing, dance, or swim, but God did bless me with the gift of Sales and Marketing. For a long time, I did not realize this was a gift. You never practice all alone in a room. You read and learn by doing. My number one rule in marketing is: If everyone else is doing it, DON'T! It seems when you work with a group the first thing everyone wants to do is see what the competition is doing and try to just follow along. No, no, no, no, no, no, no! This is what followers do, not leaders. Leaders determine what they want to see accomplished and head toward their own goal. They use vision and design the perfect event or program and accelerate in that direction.

Pricing is another area of discontent for me. A group will talk about being the cheapest. This is another series of no's from me and a group that I probably don't want to be associated with. Others want to be the most expensive with no concern for the value delivered. I say, "What would you and/or your donors be willing to pay?" If you don't know, ask. They will tell you.

At the first board meeting that I ever attended as an ED, a member arrived late, dressed as if she was getting ready to go to a garage sale and flopped her foot up on the table. She began discussing the date for their annual event which was coming up in about a month. I expressed my concern for the ability to achieve an event in this short amount of time. I will never forget her response, "We'll just throw something together." I said, "Not with my name on it, we won't!" Your name and reputation is all you have. You will be known for quality and trust in your business dealings and for your wonderful events, but a sloppy one could ruin your future abilities to attract donors. A class act does not have to break the bank, especially if you get top quality donations, free (see Wishing for Free.)

This philosophy has served me well too: Start at the top and work your way down! Why spend precious time dealing with the proper protocol. If you can directly call the President or CEO of a corporation and ask him or her to donate, or to provide goods and services, they are the decision makers! Done deal! Why would you want to spend days letting your request sit on the desk of a person that does not get things done? This can backfire on you on occasion, but it works most of the time.

This brings up the subject of "door opening!" If you don't have the top official's name, check their website. If their assistant aka "gatekeeper" screens their calls, how do you get to the decision makers? The decision maker may be the marketing person or community relations director. Ask the person that answers the phone. Listen for their name.

"Oh, hi Dave, my name is Jeanette and I'm with XYZ charity. Could you help me? I need to talk with the person that is responsible for purchasing a table for our upcoming gala." If you need a food or service donation, let them know what you need. If this is done with kindness, it is a great door opener. If you have been referred to the CEO by one of his friends or business associates, let them know. Mr. Deep Pockets is a friend of Mr. CEO and he told me that I should call him. If all else fails, and you hear he likes a particular chocolate chip cookie, send your request on the inside lid of a box with a dozen or so for the whole staff. Balloon bouquets work great, but compare the cost of the "door opener" to the amount of the potential donation. A photo opportunity with our school superintendent began with a laugh. I walked up to him laughing with my hand extended and said, "I'm the lady that has been stalking you!" He was so very busy that all these arrangements were made by his "door openers!" Be kind, be creative, but don't be pushy.

Let's talk a minute about you! Many ED's and staff members who come from the corporate world forget everything, when they enter the charity industry. They no longer feel that they have to act or dress professionally. Many feel this will make their clients feel uncomfortable; therefore they dress to un-impress. The new phrase is "de-bling" and they don't even take time for make-up or hair. Guys, you can overlook the make-up reference. In any form of selling, you must sell yourself, first. People buy from people, first, then companies and products. This applies to the charities. I always found that clients appreciated a perceived successful executive attending to their needs. This has a tendency to increase their confidence and they will take you and your advice "as gospel!" Your vendors and donors will take your requests more seriously. "Just let me meet them face-to-face and I will close the deal, if it possible!" "Jeanette aren't you being a little arrogant?" you say. Take the time to think about how you want to dress and be perceived. Be prepared. Know what you want and why they should want to help. What is in it for them? What obstacles do you anticipate? How are you going to overcome their objections? I don't rehearse an exact script, but play out the different scenarios in your mind and how you are going to close the deal or "stick the landing" like in the presentations section. You are doing a presentation to an audience of one or two. Give them the same courtesy that you would give a large audience. Remember, you are always selling. You are selling yourself, your cause, etc. to the audience of donors, volunteers, clients, etc. What do you need to fulfill your mission, and who can help you fulfill it? The bottom line of this portion of selling is: Sell yourself. If they don't buy you, they won't buy your product or give to your mission.

Sidebar on wardrobe: A very distinguished speaker was very sought after at this conference. She walked across the room and gently stroked my scarf and told me how beautiful it was. This was a black scarf with white trim and a white scarf with black trim. The scarves set me apart in a crowded convention. In wardrobe consulting, it is recommended that you pick an item you are known for. Some women wear hats, but that is a little over the top even for me. I wear a scarf draped over my left shoulder with a decorative pin. This is a good networking technique. I have met many people, mostly women by wearing my blue leopard shoes. This is not for show, well maybe a little. It is for drawing people to me to get to know them and a form of networking. My zebra dress jacket with a hot pink blouse is a current favorite.

You may say, "I can't afford an expensive wardrobe." The trick is to put all of your shirts, blouses and tops together and hang all your pants, jackets, dresses, skirts, dresses by category. Then let your imagination go wild by mixing and matching. I like to wear some evening blouses under a suit. Scarves can take the same suit and top to make a variety of outfits. Shoes can be the crowning touch. I love great shoes on sale-like jewelry never pay full price. Women, other women and donors will judge you by the bag you carry. Buy a nice briefcase and preferably a designer handbag to carry to your lunches and meetings, but it is recommended not to carry both. A briefcase at a luncheon will tell your donor or vendor that you mean business.

Let's draw on my experience as a wardrobe color consultant. Pay attention to the compliments you receive from other people. You have a tendency to wear only a portion of your wardrobe. You probably wear a certain outfit or color, because of all the positive responses you receive. Have you ever noticed people ask you if you are sick, when you wear certain outfits or colors? You unconsciously don't wear them often. The majority of colors in your wardrobe are probably the right colors for you. If you are bored someday, clean your face and pull back your hair with no color by your face. Hold up different colors next to your face. Some will add automatic color to your cheeks, lips and skin tones. Other will make dark circles under your eyes and turn your skin color yellowish, grey and take all natural color out of your cheeks and lips. It is really amazing. Again, Jeanette why are you telling us this? Remember to put your best face forward when meeting new contacts. Look your best, because people judge you within seconds of meeting you and may determine if they want to deal with you. Your grammar is also a reflection of who you portray to others. It may not be fair, but I didn't make this unseen rule and yes it is part of marketing yourself!

Successful people want to deal with other successful people and give to them. You won't forget the over six feet plus in heels, blonde lady with the pink jacket and big black bow on the shoulder. I have done follow-up and mentioned what I was wearing, and they remember. If they can't remember your name or face, they probably will remember your leopard scarf, top, and shoe with your red or beige suit. Yes, this is marketing! It has worked for me and if you will try this, let me know if it works for you.

Let's talk a minute about goal setting! This was very confusing to me when I was told to set a goal 20% below what I was sure I could produce. What? A reporter asked me once, "How do you feel about not meeting your goal?" I said, "I set my goals about double what I think I can do on a good day, therefore it's like coming in second in the World Series. I'm ok with it." This organization had never made over $15 on a similar event and I set our goal at $75,000. We raised $58,000. If I had set our goal at $20,000, we would have probably raised $21,000. As a leader if you set high goals and let everyone know that is what you need, then your volunteers and donors will work to help you meet that goal! If you try to figure this out on paper, you will see that your event probably does not have the potential to meet this goal, but this is where faith comes in. You don't believe this is marketing? You have to sell and market your goals to everyone and motivate them to help you achieve them or at least close to them. You have to believe in the best possible scenario for maximum fundraising!

Who is your Development Director or Marketing Guru? It is very odd to me that many times this is a teacher or an employee that has been with the charity and promoted to this position. A teacher told me that he loved to teach, but his school needed funds, so he was going to *have* to raise them. As I began to ask questions, he said I should write a book and encouraged me to do so! Many organization use volunteers that have never sold anything and hate to ask for donations. What are your chances for success with people who do not want to ask for money? I guess there are other "rare birds" like me, but I love to give people a reason to give to a good cause. Did you see an attitude change? You are NOT asking for you! You are not asking others to buy you a new car! You are asking for vendors, volunteers, and donors to come together and help solve a problem or nurture people in need! It's fun and easy. If someone says "No", they are just the wrong person to help you. Yours may not be a charity that they are interested in; maybe they are rich and greedy! Who knows! "No" is the number one reason, I believe, people don't like sales. I heard this story in a real estate meeting. A busy butcher shop was giving out numbers to keep the customers in sequence. The person waited patiently in line and the butcher finally called his number. The customer told the cut of meat that he needed.

The butcher said, "Next!" The customer was confused, "Why did you say, next? I have waited a long time!" The butcher said, "I don't have it, next!" Don't waste your time on people that say "no"; just say "next!"

Realtors have the possibilities to be great fundraisers. They hear "no" all the time and assist buyers (or would be donors) with the biggest purchase they have made, to date. While selling real estate I would always say, "I'm not good enough to sell someone a house they don't want to buy. My job is to find them the one they want to buy!" High pressure sales don't work most of the time. Selling the positive results of your charity will make the donor want to contribute. See the difference.

"You don't care what you sell them, just sell them something!" Where I heard this, I can NOT remember, but I remember thinking this is the rudest statement I have ever heard. The meaning is that you are not the consumer. You are the facilitator. If a customer wants to buy the ugliest house on the block, they might think it is the most beautiful home in the world. It is not your obligation to choose what a donor wants to give. Please don't "go green" in order to satisfy a funder's guidelines. If you can evolve to green and it is beneficial to your mission, then do it! Offer good solid programs and give them a choice as to which one they are interested in.

The new trend is to give to the mission and not the programs. This is the best case scenario, because donors in general do not want to give to salaries or utilities. You can make this happen by not accepting donations that are designated for a specific program. You will lose some funding. Please explain that your mission is one complete mission and your organization would like the flexibility to provide funding where necessary to operate your organization.

If you don't take credit cards, do it. Do it now. Go to your local bank and ask for the kind of account that only takes a percentage of what you bring in. Don't pay high monthly fees and don't let them sell you one of their $700 plus machines. Tell them you want a "knuckle buster." This is a credit card machine that manually swipes the credit card. The reason is that you may not have access to a phone line. You probably don't want to pay for an expensive machine. This is not free, but if your bank buys a table at all of your galas and hosts a Christmas giving tree for you, it will more than pay the fees. If they don't support you in some way, consider changing banks. Be loyal to companies that are concerned about your organization's well being. People buy more and pay more, if they can use a credit card. This includes gala tickets and auction items or just regular donations. Credit cards are a must in fundraising!

We have not talked about working with the media much. You consistently hear, "They didn't cover my event." You have to work to make this happen.
- Create an event that is unique and fun
- Create an event that aligns with your mission, if possible
- Write a press release
    1. Write one quick paragraph with color aka descriptive wording for enticement

2. Give the: who, what, when, where, why test (Is it clear?)
3. List how to register including on-line with secure credit card payment information
4. Include your charity name, contact name, address, and phone for mailing their checks
5. List sponsors with their logo for the big donors
6. Last item is to center your wonderful and informative website at the bottom (If you don't have one get one!)

- Compile a press packet
 1. Press Release
 2. Include your business card
 3. Invitation or flier of event (Tailor invitation style to event style example high-end invitations for high-end events!)

4. Updated charity brochure with no handwritten corrections, only top-quality, but they don't have to be expensive.

Please note: All this information needs to be on-line and sent in one attachment, if possible. Call the media that you want to help you. Leave a message for them with a very quick explanation of your event with date and your name and phone number. Get their email from a "gatekeeper" and send the information on-line and a follow-up hardcopy, also. This is covering all of your bases and they will see or hear of your event three times. If one or two ways is lost, you still have a chance. I have been told, "Yes, I received your information more than once!" My reply is, "I don't want to be pushy, just thorough! You are so very busy I just wanted to make it easy for you." They are usually good with this explanation. You determine where you want to be published and then how you are going to make it happen. Don't wait for them to come knocking on your door. It may happen, but probably not. This should apply to newspaper print, but pick the section and one or two of the writers for that section. In television, decide which morning shows or noon shows you want to be on. We were able to do a segment with two of our sushi chefs preparing a portion of the menu on a morning show. This is early, but many people have not left for work yet! So get up at 4 or 5 am if necessary to be there on time and prepared, plus bring a hardcopy of your press packet for the producer. Be sure to ask that your website will be shown on the screen. One Tip is always supply ample amounts of food for the crew, staff and station, even if it is sushi for breakfast. (I made that mistake only once.) They will want to have you back. Treat media like a king and they will treat your charity like a queen! A special thank you goes to Clay, Mia, Sara, Jerry, Doug, Loren, Danna Sue, and all the other dear souls that help promote the charities with our events. These are the crown jewels for all marketing endeavors. They give us freely the attention we, as charities, need for successful events.

Do not deal with "bobble heads!" These are people who shake their heads yes, yes, yes and offer to help you, but they don't have the track record for follow through. If you suspect a person may be one, test them with one task and see if they complete it. This includes vendors, donors, and volunteers. These people with good intentions will waste your time and energy. If you want to be productive and work on your marketing, programs, or other efforts, then use good time management. No matter what you have learned to this point and feel you would like to try, it all can be sabotaged by letting "users" attach themselves to you. They will use your time, energy, ideas, friends, money, etc. Beware of the "bobble heads!"

The opposite end of this spectrum is the good hearted souls that volunteer to do any job and help you, but they have no skill for the project and waste your time. Remember to let people give where they are best suited. If they cannot do the job or cannot do it well, they are wasting your time. Find them a job where they will be the most useful to your charity. If you cannot find someone to complete a task in a timely manner, then hire it done. Charities have told me how poor their website is and someone has been working on it for years, but it is free. You need a good website and you need it yesterday. Take care of it, and if you can't I have a great referral with fair pricing. "Time is money!" is the old saying that still rings true!

It has been only about nine years ago, since the words sales and marketing were almost dirty words in the charity industry. I said then and still say, "You better have sales and marketing in your charity or you will go out of business, because there are so many great causes out there for donors to give too!" You can call it whatever you want, but sales and marketing are vital to your fundraising efforts. Best wishes for becoming your own Marketing Guru!

Notes:_____

_____
_____
_____
_____
_____
_____
_____
_____
_____
_____
_____

Wish Ten

Wishing for More Fun in Fundraising!

Fun is the first three letters in fundraising, but it commonly is the last things most people want to do. I don't understand this, because it is the most fun to me. No one wants to do something that they dread. Most people say, "I hate to ask for money!" Well then, associate it with something that you like to do. What is it that you like to do? Remember, you are not asking for you. You are asking for help to continue your most valuable service to others aka your mission. Of course, this always relates back to your level of passion for your mission.

As I was trying to figure out this fundraising beast, I thought back to a time when I experienced outrageous success. My "Water Heater Queen" gig produced a statewide program that was replicated in five other states. The marketing department and the 100 seat call center had not been on very good terms. Since I was the rep over the electric water heater program in northeastern Oklahoma, it was vital that the call center understood the program and recorded all the leads for follow-up. This center answered calls for the entire state. It would have been difficult to divide the regions, therefore I asked to be over the complete program and assist the outlying reps.

Sidebar: Communications is one of the key elements for success. Many charities don't answer their phones and fail to return phone messages for up to a week. Quit being a dinosaur! Get a cell phone and roll over your calls when you are out doing errands. You could miss a call from a donor or foundation, who wants to contribute. If you don't answer, they may just go to the next charity on their call list. ANSWER YOUR PHONE AND RETURN YOUR CALLS WITH 24 HOURS OR THE NEXT BUSINESS DAY AFTER THE

WEEKEND. It is recommended to never type in all caps, because people think that you are yelling at them. I have my hands cupped around my mouth and I am yelling at you to make sure your communication is open and accessible.

I vividly remember dressing in the corporate ladies room, putting on a full length red sequin with big silver stars on the neckline and a pair of silver panty hose to compliment my silver sequin shoes. "This marketing ploy will be an outrageous success or I will lose my job in this stiff corporate environment!" I remember looking in the mirror to check my make-up and hair before I added my tiara and beauty queen sash with "Water Heater Queen" written in glitter. Now, I have to walk down the hall to the front of the call center and hope and pray for the best. I carried candy bars in a basket with my card on them. This was the ultimate example of let them know who you are and what you do. Well, to my surprise and relief, everyone laughed and smiled. Soon, they were happily eating their candy bars, smiling and thanking me for brightening their day. You see, these were underpaid, mostly single moms and college students that got yelled at on a regular basis for outages, disconnections, and over-charges on customers' bills. This is an emotionally draining job. As I looked around at a room full of 100 customer service representatives tied to their computers by their headset, I realized this was a homerun.

This was a six week promotion. These service reps could win weekly prizes by entering a drawing in exchange for one lead. The winners would be entered into a grand prize drawing. Mostly these were $25 gift cards to grocery stores and a second drawing for a large stuffed animal like an ape. It would have a sign "I'm apes about water heater leads." This was a daily reminder. Each time there was a lead the customer service rep would enter the information on a sticky note and put it on a water heater. This gave me the opportunity to follow-up for a promotional "sale." Each rep had my company cell number and they would use it regularly. The customer service reps made sure they secured every lead and had me answer any question that they couldn't answer. They connected the call to me directly. They did NOT miss a lead. I communicated with them quickly when their lead had turned into a sale. This really created strong bonds between us. Sale entries were for larger prizes with a grand prize at the end.

There were weekly contest like our "Silly Hat Contest." The woman that won was wearing a straw cowboy hat with Christmas lights on it. She plugged in at her desk. I wore a Goofy hat with long droopy ears from Disneyworld. I can't remember who won the "Crazy Shoe Contest!" I wore my stress relief shoes that consisted of two of my husband's large Crown Royal bags that were royal blue with a gold insignia. We have already discussed that I am probably not easy to live with. LOL One week we hired a clown to make balloon animals and hats for each rep. He stayed longer than he was paid because everyone was having so much fun. One week I took bubbles so they could "blow off a little steam." Another week I took king size candy bars including Paydays on payday plus a variety of other candies. One man said, "Jeanette, every week you bring us this cheap and cheesy stuff and we just love it!" This goes back to having a great attitude and remembering that it is not the cost, but the presentation.

This program concluded by netting 697 leads and 150 sales promotions in the state of Oklahoma in six weeks. Water heaters have a ten plus year life, so this limited the number of potential customers. The unexpected benefit was all the people, who desperately needed new water heaters, but could not afford them were helped. This was fantastic. We had a ball! Relations between the marketing department and the call center were strengthened. The cost of the complete promotion was around $600, as I remember. The company is still making money from the electricity used by these heaters.

Here is the final benefit. I had the opportunity to visit a few of the other call centers in other states. As I was being introduced as Jeanette North, reps would just nod with a polite hello. I would then say, "I'm the Water Heater Queen." They would laugh hysterically and shake my hand and say, "We have heard about you! Why don't you come here?" If you ever decide to pull a stunt like this for your charity, make sure you do it with a goal to connect with others that can help you achieve your goal. Do it with integrity and as much dignity as possible. Make it fun! Fun does not have to cost a lot of money, but it will pay big dividends. Done correctly, it should produce good, solid connections for future donations.

"Jeanette, this was corporate success not a charity success." The lessons that I learned from this experience parlayed into future gala success with Gala Gals having fun and helping produce profitable events. I believe that if we have to go to work every day, we might as well have fun doing it. People are attracted to a fun environment. I did not say a goofing off and careless environment. Every time you have an unpleasant task, just think about a way to make it fun.

When you need to call donors and ask for them to fund a project, figure out how many people need your help and how much it would cost to meet that need. Pick up the phone and dial it. Start with the ones that are the most receptive to your ask. A school backpack, Thanksgiving meal in a new laundry basket (these can be reused by the receiver) with a bow of course, 3 foot Christmas stocking (these cost $1 at the local dollar store) can provide fun avenues for people and organizations to give. They can see them, feel them, and touch them. They can see pictures of these gifts in the local newspaper. It is fun and people can see results. Create beautiful tickets for your galas, this will make it easier to ask for the donation and close the deal. Why call one donor for one donation, when you can call an organization or write a grant to a foundation for 25 or 50 items for your clients in need. This will add up to thousands of dollars in donations with fewer phone calls.

Fun creates enthusiasm and enthusiasm produces motivation and motivation propels actions! You may be saying there is nothing fun about my charity's issues. If you only talk about doom-and-gloom and the horrific details of your cause, you will probably run off donors. Instead, concentrate on the side of problem solving! Use the 80/20 rule. One of our favorite volunteers told me a story about his little granddaughter saying, "We are so yucky!" She named off all the good things in her young, little life and the grandfather replied, "Yes Rebecca, we are very, very yucky!" Relaying that story to a sea of donors at a fundraising event, I announced that they had the power and funds to provide all the services necessary to the poor in their community. Leave the yucky and focus on the lucky. Best wishes for more fun in all of your fundraising efforts!

Notes:_____
_____
_____
_____
_____
_____
_____
_____
_____

Wish Eleven

Wishing for Free!

Another critical step for raising money in this difficult economic environment is to find the decision makers. These are the loving and giving souls who will provide you with goods and services for FREE! By not having to pay for these wonderful donations, you are saving money that you don't have to raise in order to buy these items. For example, if you need meat for the menu at your annual fundraising gala, and there is a company in your city named <u>National Steak and Poultry</u>, don't ask them for money! Ask them for what they have, wonderful steak and tender chicken. Remember to give them the same praises and sponsorship in your media, program, and thank them publically at the event with their logo and all others on power points prior to the event. Think about what you need, write down the item and in the best case scenario what company would you want to supply this need.

My very first event was "Ultimate Spa Day" with 25% of the proceeds given to a charity. First, I need a large, beautiful room preferably with a view to hold the event. The penthouse convention room at the DoubleTree Hotel would be perfect! I did not get it for free, but at a considerably reduced fee including an eloquent lunch buffet. My Company was a for-profit with a heart for charity! Robert, the Manager, was familiar with the charity and wanted to help. Nurturing those who nurture others was the tagline. What pampers women? Think top of the head to bottom of the feet. Marshon's the former hairstylist for the Miss Oklahoma and best salon in our state would be perfect! My friends, Charles and Michael, came and brought extra stylists with them, free. I'm getting ready to go see my friend tonight to get my hair done. Charles told me a year later that some of women that he met at USD are still his clients today. His goodwill paid off in future clients and increased his bottom line. Lancôme Paris Cosmetics are the upscale cosmetics of choice in my view. Their area representative, Darcy, still works for this Company. She was a real jewel, because this was one of the very rare times this corporation went off-site for an event. They not only supplied four make-up artists but also brought the most high-end, over-sized decoration that added a real touch-of-class to the event, all free! My friend, Mary Cook, who owns Bodyworx Day Spa, is the best massage technician not only for relaxation but for pain management. She and a few other spa specialists provided mini massages plus hand and feet paraffin treatments, free. Mary also confided in me that she still has clients that were introduced to her at these events. My friend, Jeanette, provided one-on-one mini counseling sessions for women's issues, free. Michael at Body by Michael gave tips on fitness and health plus free one-on-one sessions at his gym and a free workout week. Each vendor was given time to speak about their services and gave the women helpful hints for relaxation, pampering, and products. The crowning jewel was getting to know the manager of the Godiva Chocolatier store who gave samples to every woman, free. Did you see the pattern? Friends gave freely.

I took the time to get to know these future friends and did not ask for free upfront. Offer to pay if you can, but ask for a reduced price. If you know there is no way you can afford their services, explain your charity in a nutshell, and then tell them you vision for the event. Once you land a prestigious name like Godiva and Lancôme Paris, other companies will want to be a part of your event. Explain the benefits of demonstrating their products to potential new customers. This is a wonderful marketing technique, and one-on-one solidifies future customer relationships. The second year every company returned and most of the customers. The first year we had 47 paid participants at $99 each and the second year 81. Please note the first year was one month after 9-11 and many corporations were cancelling their events. Doing damage control, I explained to vendors and customers that it was even more vital to nurture those who nurture others.

The most surprising occurrence was how the media embraced me and this event. Over a period of two years, I spent less than $600 and received over $23,000 in newspaper coverage, that I didn't even pay for. Most stories were on the front page of the major newspaper's community section. You can't even buy this space as an advertiser most of the time. The society editor embraced all of my events and told me that she liked them "…because they were unique and help non-society charities!" This is referring to charities that provide food, clothing, shelter verses the arts. I never forgot that. Now, this is free advertising, when you are given a wonderful story complete with a picture. I always ask for them to include my website. When they visited the site, there was a brochure on-line and all the news articles up-to-date. Customers aka donors were able register on a secured site complete with the ability to pay by credit card. This sounds so common, but this was in 2001. If your contact information is left out of an article, you will not be able to secure registrations for your event. Make sure and ask for them to reference your website at the bottom of the article, if possible. Please ask the reporter or producer to run as an up-coming event and not just an after-the-fact story, unless your event is at full capacity. Noonday shows at the local television station are wonderful ways to promote your event free. Determine what you need, who can supply that need, and go out there and make some new friends!

This same technique was used for my concept-to-completion "Designer Teen Camp!" Taking the concept from "Ultimate Spa Day", what could I do for teen girls? The Madonna House is a wonderful charity that helps pregnant young women. This would be a perfect fit for this charity. Matching the participants with the beneficiaries promoted giving to their peer group that has not been as fortunate.

My friend, Linda Layman-Hull, is the owner of the most prestigious modeling agency in our state and known around the world. I worked as Linda's assistant over 20 years ago and we are still friends to this day. She discovered Amber Valletta, a very famous Supermodel and I remember her walking in our agency door as a 15 year old. Linda saw her potential immediately. Linda agreed to help me with this event. This is a woman that has never earned a living except modeling and being a modeling agent since the age of 18. She has worked for Bill Blass and her models were the only ones he would use when he came to town to do a show. She worked to help our local teen girls with walking, sitting, standing, and overall posture, and with her own personal line of make-up. I could not afford to pay her what Bill Blass paid, but she was so very kind to do this for free.

We asked a former, well-known news anchor, who had been a former Miss Texas, to host the first year. Associating with known celebrities will attract attention to your event. The three of us were featured in the local community section in the most prestigious and moneyed area of our city. The picture was 6 by 8 inches on the front page, with an article that spilled over to another page. This was meant to promote my event not a stroke to my ego, but you have to be willing to be to be "front-and-center" when it comes to promoting your business or charity. The dear woman that ran this charity did not want her picture even taken, but I coaxed her into doing a few. There again, back to the rule to "Let them know, who you are and what you do!" Get your picture in every newspaper, magazine, television segment, radio interview, newsletter, etc. to promote your charity, and it is free. Don't buy advertising, but if you must, you may be able to trade an ad for a sponsorship in smaller publications.

Attract newspaper writers' attention by being creative and position yourself with prominent public figures and companies to draw attention to your cause. Get to know the writers of articles in the sections of publications where you need a story. (Press releases are covered in the Marketing Guru section.) You are not asking for you! You are asking for others to help your charity and in return you are promoting their business and the goodwill they are showing their communities.

Don't forget to mention them by name every chance you get and how they are donating their goods and services to your event in order to raise money for this charity. This is also giving name recognition to your charity and all the good works you are doing. Bailey Medical Center and a foundation were so very generous and giving to the charity that I worked with. I want to mention them, because they opened their pocketbooks for two spectacular galas and one "Ultimate Dinner Party." Bailey Medical Center provided a renowned chef, their kitchen and kitchen staff. They allowed us to bring in outside donated food items to be prepared by this staff. They purchased over-the-top ice sculptures between 3 and 4 feet tall including the Eiffel Tower and a replica of the book the "The Ultimate Life" and others. They ordered tablecloths and napkins in my choice of color and dishes and glassware, if necessary. This was an in-kind gift of $25-$30,000 just for our second gala. They allowed us to decorate the reception area and The Bistro for our "Around the World" Gala and even the outside of the hospital with flags from every country borrowed from Tulsa Global Alliance. They gave us permission for a bagpipe player to stand on their lawn and play to welcome guest. The hospital was marvelous and I want to thank them again in this book. Thank you, Dee and everyone at Bailey Medical Center. A foundation is attached to Bailey Medical Center, but is a separate entity. They provided the largest room for our dining and educational rooms for our Japanese area of the world. Reasor's Grocery Store provided fruits and vegetables for the menu. Japanese Food Express provided four Japanese sushi chefs to demonstrate and donated 1,000 pieces of sushi for this event, free. The foundation also provided video presentation services to display vendors' logos and pictures from our other events. This added such an element of grandeur and the vendors' loved it. This was at the beginning and end of each event and during non presentation times. They attended planning sessions and helped organize. I'm sure I'm forgetting to mention everything they did, but the events were fabulous thanks to their contributions, all for free. My printer, Jeremy at Sav-On Printing & Signs, has become a friend and helps me with all kinds of off-the-wall requests. He ordered a $20,000 printing machine and made sure it was there in time to print vacation pictures to the 4 by 6 foot size that I wanted. He printed all the other smaller vendor boards that were strategically placed for high visibility at the event. Jeremy gives me printing at cost if it is a custom item and many times at a ridiculously low price or free. His quality is superior, and he is so giving to organizations that appreciate him. Thank you my friend. One more person was the tent guy, Ryan, who supplied us with two 3,000 square foot tents for our Mexico and South America section of the world. He went out of his way to make this just what we needed. In exchange, I made sure that all of these sponsors were given rave reviews in every media, where time permitted, and credit in every print venue. These two guys were invited to the gala to enjoy food and beer for the evening with their dates for free. If there were any tent malfunctions, then a professional was close to solve the problem. They were happy. If people go out of their way to help you make an event wonderful and special, invite them to attend for free, if seating permits and thank them with a plaque. This is repetitive, but it is worth repeating over and over.

I have given you one of my very secret ingredients for success when you are working on a "shoe string budget!" If you can raise $58,000 and only have $2,000 in expenses, your profit margin aka fundraising donations are huge. I would put this $56,000 debt-free donation right up against about any other. The secret is securing goods and services that you need for a reduced fee or free, but this is not for the lazy fundraiser. One that just wants to buy whatever they need and take it off the bottom line. This is not for the board or ED that does not want to ask. Some people believe that I am probably told "no" a lot, but the truth is, I'm rarely told "no!" I believe in what I'm selling and I believe others will help me achieve my goal of helping others. Best wishes for free goods and services for an increase in your fundraising bottom line!

Wish Twelve

Wishing for Spectacular Events!

Would you as a small charity like to raise $58,000 dollars with only $2,000 in expenses? My first event did! My second gala raised $77,000 with $10,000 in expenses, and it was spectacular! Don't waste your time doing a lot of bake sales, car washes, garage sales and raffles, unless you enjoy working your fingers to the bone for a couple of thousand dollars. I don't do these events. Just like in real estate, you can sell a small house or a mansion, and more than likely it will be less work to sell the mansion and you will make a much larger commission. You are selling the mansion to people who have money and are willing to spend it. I was a realtor, and when you are a new agent you take the listings and sales that you can make. Looking back about 20 years, I just did not have the confidence to approach people with money to make these sales, but watched the top 10% of realtors do it on a regular basis. If this is intimidating to you, get to know someone with money and learn about how and why people give to charities.

While working a trade show in Dallas at the National Speakers Convention about seven years ago, I had the rare opportunity to meet this most unique woman. She came right up to me and said, "Do you know anyone who would like to buy a 3 million dollar condo in New York City?" I believe in dressing for success and I guess my leopard scarf caught her attention, at least that is what she told me later. My closest friends and confidants were not jet-setters or millionaires. I quickly answered, "No, not really!" We visited for a bit and I said, "It is obvious that you are here by yourself and I am here at this conference by myself, would you like to have dinner?" She said, "Why did you ask me?" I replied, "I will probably never live in New York City and how will I ever know what it is like, if I don't spend time with you?" I thought, "Jeanette, this dinner could cost you $500 by the time you rent a limo and take her to the restaurant of her choice, but you asked." She told me to meet her at 7 at the concierge's desk in the up-scale hotel that was hosting this event. She was there when I arrived, and the concierge took us up to the penthouse restaurant and called her by name often. The title doctor was added to her name, and everyone was hovering over us. We were shown to our table facing a spectacular view of the city. We enjoyed everything from cosmopolitans to dessert, and to my surprise the bill never arrived, although I offered. She was a very eloquent and beautiful redheaded woman, and it was obvious she did not look her real age, which she would never admit. She told me of her family and how her father had died in her arms. She told me that she was facing a surgery the following week and decided to have dessert, which she rarely did. She asked me about myself, and I told her of a few small accomplishments in my eyes. I'll never forget her response, "You have the three B's-brains, beauty, and balls!" I had never heard that expression, but yes I can be bold at times. I'm not afraid to ask for what I need and neither should you.

She taught me a very important lesson through a story. She said, "You will meet people that don't need money" and went on to tell me a story about Donald Trump. I quickly realized that this was not an example, but she must know the man. She explained that if Donald wanted another man to attend a charity event and donate heavily, then he would find out what that man needed. He might have a son and want a certain person at his bar mitzvah, and then Donald would arrange for that person to attend. The old saying, "You scratch my back, I'll scratch yours!" Then the donor would show up at Donald's event with the appropriate donation amount. This was huge to the success of my fundraising career, and this was before I have even discovered charities!

The last piece of advice that this passing mentor taught me was how to close a deal. She made me rehearse this line three times until I could make it believable. "I am here to facilitate YOUR success!" Better, now say it again, "I am here to facilitate YOUR success!" Now slower with more feeling, I am ere…to…facilitate…your…success!"

Do you believe me, yet? This is the reason that I wrote this book to facilitate your fundraising success! It is your job to facilitate other's success. Later, I learned that she had been a rather famous magazine editor for a well-known upscale publication and sold real estate in her later years. I knew that I would never see her again, but I never will forget her or her life lessons!

My friend, M, said, "Jeanette, can you really teach people to do what you naturally do?" I realize fundraising is not a natural activity. You must learn how to raise money and practice, practice, practice your style. Take information from a variety of sources and find what works for you. I was telling her that my husband said, "Jeanette, you can't drive up in your BMW and ask for money." My reply was "Oh, yes I can and more than likely, I will get it!" M is a former family counselor turned financial planner who said this is really not that big of a stretch. You are counseling people. She told me, "Money respects money!" I have learned that successful people want to deal with successful people or people that they perceive as successful. Back to the issue of dressing and acting professional is a must. I am so tired of seeing ED's in jeans and t-shirts driving old beat up vans that they haul donated stuff in. I wouldn't give them my money and neither will most donors or foundations. I never buy my BMW's new, but wait for some surgeon to trade up to a newer one, and I get the like new one with low miles for the price I want to pay. This pays big dividends if you are in the field of sales and marketing or fundraising. Clean up your act literally and look in the mirror. Would you give that person your money?

Now, back to the bake sales, car washes, etc. to some people these are spectacular events. As I was planning a parade, festival, and concert in a poverty stricken area fairly close to our community, I realized spectacular means different things to different people. Such as a trailer home might be a mansion to someone that has been homeless or in substandard housing. It all depends on where you come from. My spectacular is as big and bold as humanly possible. One event planner thought a church potluck was spectacular. There is no right or wrong, except when you are trying to raise money in my view. Yes, I know you can raise $1million from one person or $1 from a million people. I prefer the $1 million from one person or foundation. If you want to raise money, find the people who have money to donate!

There are workbooks available for my fundraising events "Ultimate Spa Day," "Designer Teen Camp" and soon "Gala Gals: Party with a Purpose!" "Ultimate Dinner Party" is a very exclusive event and it will need to be handled with a one-on-one consultation and personal arrangements. "Who's Taking Care of Mom and Dad?" The Seminar was designed for baby boomers who care for their aging parents. This also can be arranged with a personal consultation.

"Gala Gals" was a phrase that I heard from my sister, who is a Development Director for a charity dealing with autism in St. Louis. Basically it is building a "Dream Team!" I recruited a group of women that each had different strengths. Kayla was the volunteer coordinator. Jody is a friend that just walked into my office, and said she wanted to volunteer. She had just quit her job as a catering coordinator for a large hotel. I didn't even know what a "hot box" was, but she did. She was an angel that just dropped out of the sky. Karen was the professional decorator that decorated my friend, Amy's beautiful home and agreed to help us. Amy is the best collector of auction items on the planet, as far as I am concerned. They later founded "Community Footprints" that benefits different causes in our community. They are the best in my book! Explore what you need and then recruit the best gals (or Guys) to fill those positions. This is gold. Jeremy is the best printer anywhere that helped us with invitations, message boards and 4 foot x 6 foot photos. Yes, I have mentioned him before, but he is the best. Build your team and promote the businesses that help and give freely to you. My friend, M, said,

"Jeanette, you get it! You understand that businesses want to help you, but you promote them to other potential clients in return. You really get this and most charities don't." We own a business; therefore I understand what other business owners' need. It is not a monetary return, it is building their client base and that is what businesses need and want. Take time to go to lunch and recruit the best "Gala Gals" and vendors, and your event will be excellent! These can just be very helpful and giving (preferably rich) ladies that love to throw big parties and have nothing better to do. Target the vendors that offer the best products and services to fulfill your event's needs, but remember to promote them every chance you get! This is repetitive, but it is worth repeating!

These are some helpful questions and comments that may help you.

1. What is the premise of your mission? Do you service the poor or the arts?

2. Who is your target market, the donors that would want to give to your mission? Remember people with money have experienced grandeur. Give them the feel of a class event even if you don't spend a fortune on it! Don't be intimidated! They are just people!
3. What would they attend? Find potential donors and ask them for their advice. What would be a fun and enticing event that is not the norm to them? I heard someone say, "I don't like charity events." I quickly asked "Why?" The response was, "They are so boring and serve rubber chicken!" So I have always made sure that my events were fun and the food outstanding. Listen for what people want and DON'T want!
4. What day of the week and date would be the best? Check local calendars for conflicting events. What time of the day would

facilitate your audience? You may have to arrange this around the availability of the venue.

5. What location would be the best fit for this event and is there a location that will provide this venue for free? This is one of the most expensive costs for an event.
6. Check on liability insurance. Many times the venue's insurance will cover your event. Ask an agent.
7. What entertainment will be used? What is the atmosphere? What music will match the feel? I have hired a harpist, bagpipe player, classical trio, etc. Check with your local university's music department. Students may just play for their dinner and fun. Get references or listen to their CD. Check with your local musical union and ask for a discounted price. Get the cards of musicians from other restaurants, events,

festivals, etc. for future references. I hired a musician at a local Italian restaurant to play his accordion, but I needed French music. He said "Oh! Like this!" It was the exact song I wanted! I explained our charity, the event, and invited him and his wife to attend. I paid him $100 because I felt that he needed the money, and I thought this would be a fun night out for them. A $100 investment in a soloist may just be the crowning touch.

8. What will the menu or hors d'oeuvres consist of? Will alcohol be served? Can it be donated? Will it be free or will two drink tickets be provided? We have found giving two drink tickets to work and cash bar for additional drinks. Can outside prepared food be brought in? Will they prepare donated food items? Beautiful personal menus can be placed on each place

setting. We have been on many cruises, and they are a wealth of information on food presentation and menu items or just watch "The Food Channel."

9. Make sure to answer these questions before the invitations are printed in order to add an enticing description of the food and entertainment. Check and double check the information. Have these donated, if possible. Don't forget to add host sponsors such as the hotel that is furnishing the room, the restaurant that is furnishing the food, etc. Include a website for more information and an RSVP and return envelope with a donor level card is a plus.

10. Who will serve? Think about using local groups to volunteer with a pre-training waiter's course. National Honor Society, football and cheer teams, etc. Use older volunteers for serving alcohol and find out

what license they need, depending on state laws.

11. Who will set up the tables and clean up? Can the same volunteers be used? Get a trusted volunteer to be the volunteer coordinator. Arrange to feed these volunteers. If you are serving expensive food items, have pizzas donated for these volunteers. They would probably prefer pizza to asparagus. Be sure and list their organizations in your programs and message boards. A picture in the local newspaper is really appreciated. Appreciation certificates are inexpensive and appreciated.

12. How will you decorate? Can you find a professional decorator to volunteer their expertise to the event? Don't require them to do all the work. Use a decorating committee. Find out the earliest time for

the venue to be open for decoration. We used antique items from a decorator's market on tables with black tablecloths for one event. Another event, three florists donated per our request, one arrangement style less than 12 inches with all white flowers. These floral arrangements were sold for $35 plus dollars at the end of each event to raise additional funds. Remember to listed as sponsors and place one of their cards by their arrangement.

13. If you are having a silent auction, get a volunteer who enjoys this. By recruiting the right person for this job, your job will be so much easier. Hire a professional auctioneer for your live auction for items over a certain amount or for unique items such as balloon rides for your "Around the World" Gala! PowerPoint presentations are excellent for showing details and videos for

action items. Flash the company logos on the screen for sponsorship reinforcement.

14. Plaques are necessary to major vendors and table sponsors, except some foundations do not want them. Find out. These can even be placed on their tables as nameplates. I have seen the happy smiles as the vendors leave the event with their plaques. This will also save time and gas by not having to deliver them later in the week. Displayed in their place of business, this will continue to promote your charity and their goodwill. This is worth repeating! Today, I saw an award in a bakery that was a vinyl record with a round nameplate thanking them for their donation. Be creative.

15. Some businesses will buy a table, but do not plan to attend. Ask if you can seat media and other potential donors in these seats. Take the time to fill these seats.

16. If security is needed, sheriff departments sometimes have to do community service hours. Off duty policemen may volunteer to help with approval.
17. Parking can be an issue. A valet service may reduce their fees. Commercial buses can be hired to transport donors and volunteers to and from parking lots in more remote areas.
18. If you are considering an outdoor event, know that you have weather to contend with. Plan an alternate date or location and put it on the invitation and in the media. This will save you the day of the event.

Entering the realtor field, I decided to have a Las Vegas themed party and invite all my friends. We used play money with my picture on it that served as a business card like reminder. "Let them know who you are and what you do!" again. The day came and it was raining, probably like the day

Noah was waiting for the ark to sail. We had less than 12 people including me. My boss did show up, but it was not a success, or so I thought. My friends continually asked me how everything was in the market. What impressed me the most was when someone I knew casually remembered my party, "I felt so bad that I didn't make it to your Las Vegas party! Are you still selling real estate?" This was three years later. I realized events are for fundraising and friend raising. Events are not only for fundraising, but for awareness and to get people talking about your business.

One day I was walking and looked down to see two pennies side-by-side one was heads and the other was tails. I realized both had the same value. Just because an event does not appear successful, because of the poor attendance or weather or any other reason, enjoy the fruits of your labor and have fun. A woman told me once, "Everyone who is supposed to be here will be." I thought "No, I want everyone there." She was right. Everyone who is supposed to be at your event will be. If you can't handle risk, forget special events. If you have to know all the answers to all the questions before an event, sorry it probably won't happen.

Another day walking to my car for lunch, I was feeling rather wonderful. I had just received a substantial five figure raise. There was a woman that I perceived to be homeless. Her outfit gave it away. I decided to give her all the money in my purse. It was only a $10 bill. She said "No, I'm going down here for a job", but the rest just did not make sense. I realized that she probably had a few mental problems, also. Then, I will never forget what she said, "I have everything I need!" "Well, let me buy your lunch!" She took the money. As I walked away, I marveled. A homeless woman with mental problems had everything she needed. When things get tough dealing with the headaches of an event, I remember this wonderful woman and the lesson she taught me. If a party planning problem is the worst thing I have to deal with, I am very blessed. Then I think "Jeanette, you have everything you need!" and smile.

If you need it, can you get it donated or at a reduced price? Don't be afraid to ask. Have fun! It's a party and you have the privilege of raising funds to help others. You are blessed that you were chosen to be at this place, at this time and bring all these wonderful people together for a good cause. Best wishes for the most spectacular events possible!

Notes:_____

_____
_____
_____
_____
_____

Wish Thirteen

Wishing for a Better Board!

What business in its right mind would have 12 bosses and 3 workers? This seems to be the case for most small charities. The President calls or comes by about once or twice a month and the Secretary and the Treasurer are loaded down with most of the recordkeeping. The rest of the Board members appear once a month or quarter to use their fictitious gavels and make vital decisions on issues that they are not even familiar with. They have not even taken the time to call or come by. There are working boards and there are governing boards. The problem is, in a small charity, the board must be a working board, and that does not mean ordering the two or three overworked employees around. "Jeanette, you sound a little disgruntled!" Remember, I network. This is the case with most charities. There are usually a few good members, but they burn out. Being a board member is many times for prestige, or it just looks good on a resume or your corporate report. This is heart breaking!

It would be so helpful, if I could report to you that Boards are wonderful and a real asset to most organizations, but that just doesn't seem to be the case. After 22 months of blood, sweat, and tears plus thousands of prayers, I was fired by the board. This was the board of the same organization that was $10,000 in debt when I arrived. This was the same organization that could not afford to even pay an Executive Director and was getting ready to be put on probation by their national funding source. I knew it was coming because of their blatant lack of participation in our gala the previous month. This firing came one month after the event to make sure all the money was collected. This left them a very hefty bottom line of approximately $200,000 in the bank plus about

$100,000 of in-kind that was never recorded. God had blessed us tremendously! There were more volunteers than there were positions and good relations within the two communities including great media bonds. One television station aired 11 stories in 11 months about our charity. My heart was broken!

I went into reclusion to re-evaluate this experience. It was time for me to go. I had learned my life lessons and helped as many people as possible. There was an extreme "red flag" warning within the first month of my accepting this position. A city official and board member said, "I don't care if this stays an impoverished charity." You see, this city took great pride in being a city where everyone made $80,000 a year or more and all lawns were perfectly manicured. They did NOT want poor people in their city. With no social services or very limited ones, everyone that needed food, utility assistance, etc.

would have to travel to the nearest largest city. Think about it, there would no longer be a record of the number of poor people and definitely no awareness in the media of what was perceived as negative press. I think that helping others is good press and you live in a fairy land, if you believe that there are no poor people in your city.

You may be giving your life blood for your most sacred mission, just be aware that others may have a counter interest in its success. While discussing this scenario with an experienced member of other charity boards, he said, "You can't put a Band-aid on cancer!" Poison will spread, therefore it is crucial to remove negative members from your boards. New members had been recruited, but the poisonous one had remained and added one more equally venomous cohort. This group of new recruits was soon pumped with power. They were making decisions based on peer pressure and the philosophy that it is better to be popular than right.

Please note that most of these people were good productive citizens in the community, they just weren't familiar with the interworking components of a board. I had cried out for help to more experienced ED's, but they saw "the writing on the wall!" They knew that this was going to end poorly. The number one suggestion was for Board Development courses. The problem with this solution is the more experienced sabotage ringleader would somehow make sure this did not happen. He would guide the board. Do not be fooled that the President is the leader of the Board. Maybe they sport the title, but do not necessarily run the board. I do have to brag on one community leader that I recruited early and told him of the issues. He resigned from the board the day I was fired and was a trusted mentor, although he had to stay inconspicuous due to his organization and its relation with the city. Remember how I said that I wasn't in politics.

Yes, you are if you run a charity that deals in social change!

Thanks for letting me get this off my chest, and now on to the fundraising aspects of a board. They must give. Even if you have clients on your board, $1 a year is fine. The Board should give and connect you to their sphere of influence aka friends and business associates with deep pockets. They should connect you to their corporation's community relation director. In leadership books they refer to building a "Dream Team." This was the concept for my recruitment. Here is the problem. An ED should not be responsible for Board recruitment. The Board should be the recruiters. I know as the ED it is beneficial to have friends on the panel, but this is not your job. A lazy board will tell you who to recruit and sit back and criticize. Back to the teambuilding side of boards, I would recommend, one mover-and-shaker from different industries. Look for one, bank president, realtor, restaurateur, CPA, attorney, politician (be careful), media source, various large corporation executives, technology, education, clergy, and make sure and throw in some rich people with kind hearts and preferably retired! This sounds like a recipe for success. Just make sure to leave out the poisonous snakes, they can ruin the whole mix!

"Jeanette, you're off on board recruitment not fundraising!" Recruitment is foundation building for fundraising! You must have board members that have the ability to give and will give. I feel another story coming on. Sitting in a make shift board room with just enough members for a quorum, I was giving a presentation of my vision for the upcoming first gala. The invitations had already been printed with the ticket price on them of $100 each. I will never forget this statement, "These will have to be reprinted, because WE don't want to pay that much!" Raise the "red flag", now! They went on to explain that $100 tickets and $1,000 tables had never been sold in our city. I had already sold about 20 tickets and a couple of tables. No one told me this was not doable! I was frustrated. This board would not raise money and we needed money. Of all the things charities need the most-money is the number one thing! This is my battle cry. From my small little salary, I contributed more to the galas than they did on an individual basis. I contributed more on a yearly basis then they did. I was one of their donors!!! I don't say this to give myself a pat on the back; I say this to emphasize they were NOT doing their job! I was doing my job and was expecting no more than that from them. "Calm down, Jeanette!" I felt the love. I felt the passion for the mission. If you are a board member and don't feel a burning love or passion for the mission, leave. Please go back to the corporate world and peddle your "dead man walking" attitude there. Oh! Sorry I'm supposed to be nice, but I get like a mother bear looking out for her cubs, when someone is hurting a charity and therefore hurting people in need.

The bottom line of fundraising is collecting an ample amount of money to fulfill your mission of helping others. Maybe this section should have been called "Wishing for a miracle!" There are good people out there with good hearts serving on thousands of boards. My sincerest "thank you" goes out to you for your service. Sometimes examples of "what not to do" will give you the knowledge to ward off potential disasters. Best wishes for recruiting a great board that will participate and monetarily support your mission!

Notes:_____

_____

_____

_____

_____

Wish Fourteen

Wishing for a Miracle!

You may wish for a magical solution to your fundraising, but I prefer miracles! Many people do not believe in modern-day miracles, but I do. If you work with charities long enough, you will hear the most amazing stories. One day another worker, a volunteer, and I were in the food pantry and I said, "I wish we had more toilet paper!" It is obvious that if a family cannot afford food, then they cannot afford the necessaries such as toilet paper, shampoo, soap, cleaning supplies or pet food. Food and these other items were rarely purchased from our budget. I believe that most communities want to take care of their own citizens, and if they are made aware of the needs they will respond. Be sure to work closely with your local television stations and newspapers when you are in need, because these are great human interest stories for slow news days. Be ready with a recent story of need and a program to promote on a minute's notice. Oh! You want to hear about the miracle. Scout groups and church teen groups would usually respond quickly to these needs. Within a few weeks, there was a real commotion at our door. I took off out of my office to hear about some teen groups that had challenged each other in a contest that I knew nothing about. They were ready to unload about 6,000 rolls of toilet paper and other non food items. We had rented a few extra rooms for an upcoming project and this donation filled one room to the brim and at least 6 feet high! "Oh Jeanette, this was not a miracle, but a coincidence." Ok, I'll give you that one, but read about this one and tell me what you think!

If you hang around me very long, you WILL hear my nun story. I had the good fortune to meet a Nun while volunteering for another charity. She needed a ride to the airport and I happened to be going that way, so off we went in my silver BMW roadster convertible with the red leather interior. This is probably not something you see every day. As you have probably noticed, I am not a very conservative person. We connected on this short ride in spring of 2005. Fast forward to summer 2007. I am on my way to buy a wedding gift at an upscale discount store and planned to be there by noon. Everything happened that could happen to detain me, and I arrived about 3 pm. As I was shopping I noticed a woman and wondered where we had met. Oh! It was the lady from the charity, and I asked her about this Nun. She pointed a few aisles over and said, "She's right there!" Now this is a nun from Texas, visiting a friend in Tulsa, shopping in our small town at the exact same time I was. She said, "Jeanette, how are you doing?" I said, "Oh Sister, I just started working for a smaller charity similar to the one she worked with. There are so many needs and they have no money.

I just don't know what I am going to do!" She took my card and gently rubbed the top and put it in the small purse hanging where a name badge would. She said, "Maybe we can give you a grant." The following Sunday, I emailed her saying that God had brought us together for a reason, and what did I need to do to start this grant process. I didn't receive a return email, but knew that she was a very busy woman. I heard that she was one of the first three people into the Astrodome to begin the set-up for the massive relief shelter after Hurricane Katrina.

A few weeks later, I went to our charity's big, black mailbox, and to my surprise there was an envelope from The Sisters in Texas. I quickly open the envelope and to my elation there was a check for $2,000. Well, I thought it was $2,000 until I put on my reading glass and saw it was substantial five figure donation. I never even filled out a grant request.

There is a part two to this story. About ten months later, we held our second annual "needs" forum and invited in all the churches. There are 55 churches in our city of 35,000 people. The sad part of this is only about 10 actually gave to our cause and participated in this forum. We estimated about $85,000 was needed to meet all the demands of our clients in our community at the time. I set high goals to meet maximum need. Please do the same. I watched as their eyes rolled back in their heads as they heard this figure. Most of the larger churches were not represented. I told this group of mostly mission outreach leaders, "I'm going to tell you what I tell some of the little, old ladies that call. They say that they are too old to volunteer and don't have much money, what can I do? I ask them, "Can you pray, because that is what we need the most?"" Ten days later, I went back to the same mailbox and saw an envelope from The Sisters in Texas. I opened a check for another substantial five figure donation that we did NOT even ask for! This was only 10 months after we had received the first check and donations are rarely given within the same year. As my friend Margaret always says, "God is Gooooooood!" Now this is my kind of fundraising! It is easy and I never even filled out one form.

People sometimes ask me, "Jeanette how do you fill out a grant?" It's like filling out a real estate contract. My national funding source request took me forty hours the first time I "over" did it. I rarely fill out grant requests, because when we need something, I just ask people to pray for it and it comes! I was told one of the most difficult foundations to get approval from had to have every "I dotted and every T crossed!" You needed to go on-line, and it was a very formal and structured process. I just wrote a letter and made a request with simple facts and figures to the decision maker of the foundation. I remember smiling as I sat in the introductory interview, after we had already received the money and never even put my name on or filled out a grant form. Again, this can backfire on you, but sometimes God grants us our request. "Ask and you shall receive. Seek and you shall find. Knock and it shall be opened!" I call this wisdom-ancient sales and marketing advice. Believing is a key element.

The best advice is when you have a true need for funding; ask people to pray first and then proceed, instead of taking off with a project or event and then asking God to help you. It is better to help God with his work on this earth! This is the true secret to my success, and it can be the answer to your fundraising needs. My dad used to say, "Some people think God is a Santa Claus for every little want." I say, "Respect your Creator and believe that he will supply all of your needs and those of your charity." Praying for a miracle is better than wishing for a miracle, any day!

Notes:

Wish Fifteen

Fundraising is More Than Wishing!

This all began with a Moroccan fundraiser and my decision to make a genie costume. I kept thinking pink then remembered a pink satin evening gown in my closet with a beautiful sheer white overlay with bugle beads. This had been part of my cruise ensemble and never fit just right. With a pair of scissors, iron, sewing machine and 75 hours, this wonderful costume only cost me $75.

This was to be a corporate party for a friend's clients, but I ask her why not make it a fundraiser. She found a local church that was taking a mission trip to Morocco and they not only needed money, but were taking clothing. I found about 40 adorable "onesies" at the local dollar store that were perfect. These are wonderful sources for many charity needs. We had a costume contest and each vote cost $1. We received over $700 that evening without really trying. The first place trophy was a leather camel mounted on a trophy base with a recognition plaque. This camel was on sale half off for $12.99 at Hobby Lobby and the mount and plaque were about $10. This provided a marvelous award for under $25. Network with local merchants and tell them your needs such as inexpensive trophies for your charity events. Scoreboard was so kind to let me shop in his "bone yard" where bits-and-pieces of mismatched trophies where scattered. He always gives me a good price and even attached a pink poodle for a recent 50's event. This was a Christmas ornament from a local craft store. Don't be afraid to go "kitschy!"

After being fired from my first ever Executive Director's position with a charity that I dearly loved, this was my "sewing therapy." The irony of this story is that it almost landed in the trash a few times, when I felt very, very frustrated. While trying to design something without a pattern, it took perseverance and more than one effort to make it work. The top did not want to stay in place, so I found an old strapless bra as a firm foundation and pinned it on until it achieved just the right shape before attaching. I lovingly refer to the fancy fringe on the midsection as genie the "later years!" You see, a ball gown with a little vision and effort can be restructured into something new and wonderful as long as you have a good foundation and don't give up. Now, go out there and create your new and wonderful organization that will attract ample funding for your most precious mission! It is the complete package of a solid business structure tying it all together with the beautiful, big gold bow of passion. Best wishes and remember that fundraising is more than wishing!

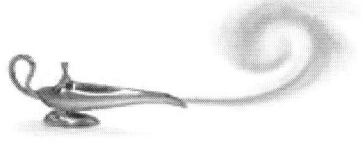

About The Author

Jeanette North has a proven track record of success in the field of sales and marketing for over 20 years. As the Executive Director of a charity, fundraiser and special event planner, she revitalized a charity moving funds to $212K in 22 months. She planned and executed two fundraising events that resulted in over $135K with expenses less than 9%. Over 4,000 individuals were served across two cities through her recruitment efforts of volunteer groups. Jeanette spearheaded public transportation through partnerships, and they received the largest federal grant of its type in the state in 2007. Through partnerships, she helped secure a $50K foundation grant for Domestic Violence Intervention Services (DVIS) and Parent Child Center counseling services for four cities. Under her leadership, this organization received 176% increase in United Way funding in 2008. Knowing that her work was blessed by God, this was all accomplished in 22 months.

Jeanette was the Chairwoman for a large charity's NeighborFest '05 and volunteered approximately 700 hours. This included coordinating a parade, festival and concert. She founded NorthStar Productions, LLC that designed concept-to-completion events and seminars including "Ultimate Spa Day", "Designer Teen Camp", and others. Jeanette North believes in relationship building, partnerships and networking. She has worked with Godiva Chocolatier, Lancôme Paris Cosmetics, Dillard's, Belk, Linda Layman Modeling Agency, F&M Bank, RCB Bank, Anheuser Busch Sales of Oklahoma, Bailey Medical Center, Reasor's, Fox 23, KTUL Channel 8, KJRH Channel 2, Radio Disney, Tulsa World, and many other foundations, corporations, churches, schools, charities, and others.

In May 2009, Jeanette received her Bachelor of

Science in Organizational Leadership and was named Distinguished Graduate ORGL for the School of Business at Rogers State University in Claremore, Oklahoma. The Rotary Club of Owasso awarded her the Service Above Self-Nicaraguan Water Well Project- 2008. The Owasso Chamber of Commerce presented her with the Community Impact Award- 2007. Jeanette was active in the Tulsa Area United Way's Agency Speakers Bureau and received the 42nd Street Award-2006. She received the "Rookie of the Year" from Prudential Properties of Oklahoma in 1991.

Jeanette North can be reached at 918-902-1154.

Works Cited

21 February 2009 <http://www.en.wikipedia.org/wiki/I have a dream>.

21 February 2009 <http://en.wikipedia.org/wiki/Gettsburg_Address>.

20 February 2009 <www.tonyrobbins.com>.

20 February 2009 <http://www.nsaoklahoma.org>.

20 February 2009 <http://www.hookedonsafety.com>.

Adler, Ronald B. and Jeanne Marquardt Elmhorst. Communicating at Work. New York: McGraw-Hill Companies, Inc., 2008.

Agnes, Michael, Charlton Laird and Staff. Webster's New World Dictionary and Thesaurus. New York: Simon & Schuster, Inc., 1996.

Brantley, Clarice Pennebaker and Micjhele Goulet Miller. Effective Communication for Colleges. Mason: Thomson South-Western, 2008.

Famous Quotes. 21 February 2009 <http:famousquotes.me.uk>.

Irwin, Richard. "The Keys to an Effective Oral Presentation." Times Mirror Higher Education Group, Inc. 1996.

McGlasson, Debbie. Director of Pelivan Transit Jeanette North. March 2007.

Plummer, Sara. "City of Owasso, Pelivan Transit: Officials debate public transportation grant." Tulsa World 4 July 2007.

—. "Owasso City Council: Public transportation plan OK'd." <u>Tulsa World</u> 19 September 2007.

—. "Owasso explores options for public transportation." <u>Tulsa World</u> 25 April 2007.

—. "Ticket to ride, Popularity of Pelivan Transit in Owasso grows after first month." <u>Tulsa World</u> 30 January 2008.

Staff, writer. "$120,000 grant awarded for Owasso transit service." <u>Owasso Reporter</u> (2007).

Stovall, Jim. 21 February 2009 <http://www.jimstovall.com>.

Stovall, Jim. <u>President, Narrative Television Network</u> Jeanette North. August 2001.

<u>The History Channel.</u> 2009.

<u>The Ultimate Gift.</u> Mechanicsburg: Executive Books, 1999.

Velasquez, Manuel G. <u>Busines Ethics Concepts and Cases.</u> Upper Saddle River: Pearson Prentice Hall, 2006.

Walters, Dottie and Lilly Walters. <u>Speak and Grow Rich.</u> Paramus: Prentice Hall, 1997.

Whited, Jerry. "Council renews Pelivan Transit's agreement." <u>Owasso Reporter</u> 21 August 2008.

Wilder, , Lilyan. <u>7 Steps to Fearless Speaking.</u> New York: Wiley and Sons, 1999.